Mustard Seeds

Their Stories: American College Students Today

Mustard Seeds:

College Students Today

Michael Abramovich

Frederic Beacham

Matthew Bush

Meghan Cohanan

Matt Coombs

Zana Ismail

Gabriella Leone

Olivia Porch

Rosanna Santangelo

Mark Seskin

Patrick Slyman

Terence Sullivan

Crystal Talbot

Dana Vecchiarelli

ISBN: 1482325845
ISBN-13: 9781482325843

TABLE OF CONTENTS

MUSTARD SEEDS

> He said, "How will we liken the Kingdom of God? Or with what parable will we illustrate it? It's like a grain of mustard seed, which, when it is sown in the earth, though it is less than all the seeds that are on the earth, yet when it is sown, grows up, and becomes greater than all the herbs, and puts out great branches, so that the birds of the sky can lodge under its shadow."
>
> — Mark 4:30–32

Olivia Porch's powerful and unforgettable poem "Upon a Mustard Seed," is even more powerful and unforgettable when you know the experiences, hers and her friends' at the College of Staten Island, that gave rise to such feelings of anguish and transcendence. There were few easy days in their schooling in a society dedicated to squeezing every nickel out of public education, a system designed to drain the spirits of students before they find the teacher, the book, the subject that can nurture their seeds of potential into growing minds and souls.

Books abound about today's college students, but they are written by professors and other professional educators. Their favorite parable about education is probably not the mustard seed, but the story about the sower who blames the failure of the seed to take root on the poor soil, or, as one of Jim Bouton's managers put it, "I managed good but they played bad."

This book is written by college students, writing about themselves. Their stories are uplifting and upsetting, and they do not pull their punches. They have earned the right to give testimony: like Walt Whitman, they can say, "I am the man; I suffered. I was there."

This book grew out of my senior seminar for history majors at the College of Staten Island. They read the *Education of Henry Adams*, a book unmatched in its cynicism about the value of formal education. But while they understood the reasons for Adams' cynicism, to a person they rejected it. They are under no illusions about the failings of public higher education, but they also see its value, at least its potential value. But enough preface. Let them speak for themselves.

Richard Gid Powers

PROLOGUE:

UPON A MUSTARD SEED

By Olivia Porch

I was a seed never watered,
Never given intellectual nourishment,
Trying to grow in an environment not meant for me.
Born into a world that's confused
Twitching and turning in a seat, this means I have a
learning disability?
Confused world, I am amused world. You have no clue
world what to do with a child like me.
Your answer was to give me a disability called ADD, an
enemy that I had to defeat.
ADD based off of subjective criteria,
Psychiatrists, teachers, who are you to spread such a
disease.
Thanks to you I became the experiment that I never
wanted to be.
The environment haunts, leaving scars such as grade
marks
The ghost of education's past came to warn
That some teachers and the complete educational sys-
tem have done children wrong.
It devastates total masses taking away their strength

Weakening, creeping into the spirit ripping the heart
from where it belongs
Children learn early whether they are a failure or not
due to labels.
From elementary to college the grades don't stop,
grades are lies they're not stable
Since I was young I knew I was able.

My age continues to rise I hear the clock, tick tock tick
tock
Finally I have arrived at CUNY and ask myself what do
I think? Do you really want to know?
I gave it a shot
Everything I thought it would be it was not.
Like elementary and secondary education it leaves you
in the same spot
Crippled, fearing the world with no clear vision,
It manipulates your own intuition
Listen
You should be seeking yourself
Your strength, abilities this is the true mission
Find self-definition.
CUNY continues to put you in a spirit ripped, mentally confused, heartless condition.
After CUNY is done it spits you out, abandoned, jobless with no position.
Do not be surprised this is tradition.
Those who accomplished completely, doing what they
loved to do, dropped out of school, no college.
They found peace and accomplishment in their own
self –knowledge.

Thomas Edison produced over one thousand
inventions
Kicked out of school because he could not pay
attention
Not to mention
Abraham Lincoln was president of the United States
no degree
He signed the emancipation proclamation setting the
slaves free
He sits in the national mall in Washington D.C
Forever remembered throughout history.
Walt Disney created a land of joy, imagination, movies
with creativity
For all ages no discrimination
Leaving behind his own legacy for generations
No college education.
Albert Einstein genius physicists through hard work
and dedication
He said "The only thing that interferes with my learning is my education."
He failed tests, no stress. He overcame the system
teaching himself in many different ways.
No shame
He saw his purpose his own vision
Looked upon as a failure, Einstein brought out the self-knowledge inside that was hidden.
Bill Gates went to Harvard but had a change of heart.
A prestigious college he could have graduated from but
he did not
The question everyone should ponder is whether a
degree makes you smart?
For Bill he showed the world that labels do not make
you who you are

Getting a piece of paper did not make him or break
him
Cause in the end he found his abilities believing he
would make it.
College can take you but only so far.
It's as if you're a hitchhiker and when you graduate it's
time to get out of the car.
The time you spent inside confined left you blind with
no direction
Finally you start to have some self-reflection.
Seeking your talents, what you love, how to make the
impossible come true.
College teaches you from a very narrow point of view.

So what happened to the seed, did it ever grow?
What gave the seed water, intellectual nourishment?
I really want to know.
It was removing the negative labels that manifested
itself in my life
Learning how to teach myself, putting CUNY aside
Why did I have to pull myself out of the CUNY insti-
tution to actually learn?
I took off a year, time to share what I discerned
Professors with no compassion
Molding the brain by a standard
That for some creates a negative reaction
Grades, GPAs make students unequal
If you have a 2.0 you're banned from entering honor
society clubs
Now this is truly evil.
Who believed that grades and marks make you smart?
Who implemented such a rotten system from the start?
The 2.0 student could be intellectual in so many ways

Instead they're looked at as slow, incapable just because
they don't have the highest grades?
I'm not done
What happens to the 4.0 student who masters every
CUNY class?
Where is he now? I think it's time we asked?
Well he applied for every job he could think of, he
started not to care
He would take anything even if it was a hard job he
had to bear
He busted his hump, day and night studying, getting
the highest grades.
You start to see the 2.0 and 4.0 CUNY student both
deal with inequality in different ways.
It does not fade
The social class structure remains the same
The system is made so you compromise your life for
any job that will pay
Thomas Edison said "Every man makes his own salary"
Could we say this is true today?

CUNY is stamped majority poor and middle class
that's why it's not respected
Those students whether 2.0 or 4.0 most get rejected,
Neglected
The marks, grades labels it is not what you need.
The ultimate knowledge is your-self, your worth, your
purpose.
The faith the size of a mustard seed
So as for Thomas he is right, the salary is yours
As for me getting a degree is just a societal chore
Without it most of your opinions are ignored
So in order to change education, heal it

You have to become the cure
Take out all of the problems all the way to its core
I have just shared my own knowledge to the world of a system
That should be completely reformed
From the bottom up stop creating inequality for the American student
If you see they have problems in science, math, English don't stand there give them an F
Take time out to improve them
Professors, teachers you have to understand, your job is noble like a nurse in a hospital unit.
Every child counts they all have different ways of learning,
Sit down master your students
No excuses
Though every professor, teacher is not like this but one is too many
Infecting a student's life with discouragement is very deadly
There is no room for error
You're dealing with a human being, spirit, his soul
The infection is some professors, some teachers, the exams, grades,
The system as a whole
Jesus is god who came down as a man long ago
He gave so many passages of encouragement, telling man he can achieve the impossible
Faith is important it is a gift
It's hard to fulfill your own purpose without it
So stand up tall declare you believe in yourself
By doing just this you have all the riches and wealth

The wealth that does not exist in school or money just
to look in the mirror and not have to ask
Who are you? You've figured it out, education is life
experience, your dreams, everything you want
pursue
Those who have made it completely, fulfilled a degree
or not are very few
Think about that thought and look inside of you
My mustard seed has grown, it's developed the sky's the
limit
Finally college is over, school is finished
Life continues I'm out of prison
Hopefully, I'll help other students or individuals whose
dreams have been diminished

I'm not bitter nor angry I'm just breaking, exposing
cracking the CUNY shell it's been long overdue
Whether you agree or disagree I'm sharing my personal
view
Allowing the reader to walk in my shoes

CHAPTER 1:

MICHAEL ABRAMOVICH

I look at my essay and consider my experiences, and I reflect on what made me who I am today. I realize that it was adversity that has shaped me. Social and academic challenges taught to me always to push myself and strive to be better and stronger. I would never be able to appreciate anything I managed to accomplish if it had come without work. It was the blood, sweat, and effort that made me capable and resilient.

Most importantly I value life experiences equally as much as educational experience. I bear witness to the fact that academic experiences and real life experiences depend on each other in producing a completely well rounded individual. Education provides knowledge to the student, while real life experiences are enhanced by academic knowledge. With real life experience, the student becomes the teacher, and can pass on that knowledge.
M.A.

THE EDUCATION OF MICHAEL ABRAMOVICH

When people ask me about my education; I ask them if they mean my formal education or my real education. To a person of true intellectual worth, education goes beyond the classroom. I have always found that the classroom always held only a limited knowledge in its walls, and most teachers are as imbecilic as the students they are trying mold to a standard that is of no value in the world beyond school. The idiots who run the education systems today feel that all a child needs to learn to be functional in society is to read, write, and do basic mathematics. While these are important, I believe that civics, creating a love of learning beyond the classroom and teaching young minds how to think for themselves have as much importance as reading, writing, and math. After all, what is the point of learning how to read when a person develops no personal initiative to read when he doesn't have to? It is obvious that very few people read for pleasure, or have any interest in learning beyond the classroom.

If I were to discuss my education in my own way I would talk about what influenced me to take the cognitive path I'm on today. My education holds great value to me in that it led to come to conclusions and understandings that shaped the lens that allows me to see what I see today. A lot of my views can easily be compared to Henry Adams' whose outlook could be termed very cynical. The education I received allowed me view things in a very harsh, critical, and what I consider realistic way. Although I admire idealism, I have found idealists get lost and disappointed by the truth of things, and therefore I have come to my conclusion that humanity for the most part has acted out of selfish greed, and the good in people is very limited (and is not without its own selfish intentions). I will explain how these conclusions came to fruition and why I accepted them.

It is important to understand that my formal education started before I went to school. My mother and grandmother tried to teach me how to do mathematics at the age of four (a year before I stepped into a classroom). My mother also emphasized the importance of learning to read and write. As an immigrant who had to learn English quickly and apply it in college she understood the value of being linguistically fluent to achieve assimilation. As a child not native to the United States (I was born in St. Petersburg Russia, and came to the United States at the age of three) I had to pick up the American language and culture to fit in. Most of it came from TV where pop culture quickly sucked me in.

In the classrooms of the public education establishment I was the outsider from day one. From as early as Kindergarten I hated school. First, I didn't know English as well as everyone else, and had to take ESL (English as a Second Language). Secondly I was very shy, and very timid; therefore I could not make friends (my neighborhood friends went to a different public school in the area).

By second grade I was excelling academically (due to the push to study at home from my mother and grandmother, and an amazing teacher who was patient and encouraged me to show her what I was capable of). At the end of that year I tested out of ESL and was put in advanced classes. But as much I excelled in academics, I believe I didn't learn much of anything that could be considered of true value. I scored in the top 10% in the math, English, and science. But I always did terribly with history, a subject I had little affection for.

However the true education I received was from my peers. They weren't fond of a kid who was different. Being pushed around taught me to be resilient. But another lesson I learned very well is that people around me were cruel, worthless pieces of work. I found later on that they were dunces, worthless individuals who lacked the ability to understand someone who thought abstractly. Nevertheless I followed my teachers' wishes and so as a kid I always tried killing people with kindness.

When I was twelve I moved to Staten Island and once again was received as an outsider by the same crowd of brain-dead fools. For the first time I made "friends" at school but soon learned the difference between fair weather friends and people who fit the meaning of the word. Once again I found myself the subject of torment and ridicule by my peers while refusing to fight back out of a regard for authority. But I kept learning how to deal with hardship and how to endure.

High school was where I really started my true education. The Marine Corps Junior Reserve Officers Training Corps (MCJROTC, or ROTC as it was called) was where I began learning everything I needed to know. For once I had a place where I belonged (a good portion of the guys were social misfits as well), and the idea of serving seemed like something fun and cool to do. By this time I had gone from being a good student in general to a terrible student in the math and sciences and an outstanding student in history and English. I found that I loved the studies that helped understand human thought and human actions, and I knew that any studies I'd pursue would be associated with these.

How I dealt with my idiotic peers also changed when I was in high school. My JROTC upper-classmen taught me to fight back. They reminded me that there was nothing wrong with striking those who gave me a hard time, or pushing them down a flight of stairs as long as a teacher or administrator didn't see me do it. I also learned that very few thugs dared to accept a challenge to a fist fight after school (most of them couldn't even take a single hit). I made sure the imbecilic thugs who were looking for a victim to pick on stayed clear of me unless they were looking for a beating. This tough attitude is what kept four years of high school peaceful for me.

The events of September 11, 2001, left a mark on me and locked me into the idea of service in the military. From that time on I had a great desire to protect my country from all enemies foreign and domestic. I cared very little for academics except English and history, and focused on training in the JROTC. I would graduate with pride and a desire to sign an enlistment contract with the US military.

At the age of eighteen I signed my contract for the US Army National Guard for the state of New York and was fully ready to deploy to Iraq. After spending a brief semester at CSI I shipped out to Initial Entry Training to become trained as a Paralegal Specialist (a job I was pushed to take because of my score on the Armed Service Vocational Aptitude Battery [ASVAB-the military's aptitude test]).

My education as a soldier began by breaking down all the rules and norms society had taught me in my first eighteen years, while I was indoctrinated in a way of life very few dared to take on. I faced the harsh reality that sooner or later I would find myself in Iraq, and I needed to absorb everything my Drill Sergeants could teach if I wanted to have a chance of survival. I learned the basic technical knowledge that let me understand the Army equipment a GI would have to use. The physical training and training in the field taught me that my mind could endure more than I thought it could. It was this education that gave me the will always to seek a challenge and never quit. I remember very little about my specialty training aside from long classroom days learning the basics of military law and what I had to do. When I came back, I would see the academic world through slightly different set of eyes.

When I went back to college I wanted to avoid being on Staten Island (and avoid days of work at a retail job I loathed with terrible pay). I decided to go to John Jay because I thought Forensic Psychology would be a fun major. However I quickly formed a hatred for John Jay and only liked my history and classical literature classes. The papers I wrote for those classes were nothing noteworthy and nothing I ever bothered saving. I only saw them as long homework assignments and a waste of time. The only paper I ever recall that showed some true brilliance and the beginning of my superior awareness was a paper for my Ethnic studies class. In that paper I explained how my old neighborhood in Brooklyn changed and where it was going. I also unconsciously wrote of my hopes and fears about the neighborhood where I spent the early years of my childhood. Like most college students of nineteen and twenty I was not sure of what I wanted out of my education. I found myself lost in an uncertain world and spending time I could only call the wasted years.

My deployment to Iraq was an eye opening experience and a further education in life experience. While I will not dwell on specifics, I will say that words cannot explain something that clings to you forever. I was stationed on Camp Bucca, a base located in the south of the country. It was a prison base where captured insurgents from the north were sent. As a military paralegal I expected to do the job I was trained for. But I was still a soldier in a warzone. I found myself disgusted with careerist officers and sergeants who constantly put themselves above their soldiers. They were disgusting individuals who were willing destroy their own subordinates for the sake of career progression. I called them Blue Falcons (slang term meaning Buddy Fuckers). I felt more times than a few that the enemy was wearing the uniform that said US Army rather than the insurgents in the Theatre Internment facility or the Insurgents outside the base ready to blow us to bits.

The other important thing I learned from Iraq was that the media and the pundits who talked about this war were full of it. As a soldier with boots on ground I saw the truth. I met the people, and I saw what the soldier experienced. We were the experts because we lived and breathed there. The idiots who were PhDs or held some title of respect knew nothing. No amount of book knowledge could equal true and raw experience.

Returning to civilian life, I came back as someone who now had superior knowledge. I was above being influenced by the simple minded morons around me. I was ready to go back to college, and this time to learn the skills to present an accurate story that would make people understand the truth.

I never expected the experience I received when I came back to CSI in the fall of 2008. I met professors in the history department who weren't pompous idiots who believed they were always right, but instead individuals who were willing to teach me how to make my views clear and well presented. I loved my classes and learning about a world which was bigger than me. Everything I learned I integrated into my views, and my views were still shifting and still evolving.

One of the most important courses in my development as a historian was American Cultural Studies with Professor Lavender. We looked at art and music that were affected by society's influence on the individual. One of my masterpiece papers at the time was my discussion of the graphic novel *The Watchmen*. My reason for writing about it was that *The Watchmen* was the product of 1980s culture and the Cold War. It also changed comic book culture in that it broke apart the super hero mythos (selfless, powerful individuals always above the human consciousness, doing the right thing and being loved for it). It wouldn't be until later on that I realized this as an important point that I always knew but never fully cognitively processed.

The course that was most important in my development as a historian was History 300 with Professor Haj. It was in her class that I perfected my views, and gained the ability to articulate my thoughts and ideas in a viable product. Some of her assigned readings of E.H. Carr and Michel-Rolph Trouillot had a significant impact on my understanding of history. Having read Carr before taking Professor Haj's class I already understood that history had a level of subjectivity to it. It was Trouillot who showed me how those who held power produce knowledge the way they wanted. It was the theories of Michel Foucault and Jacques Derrida that helped fully form my views. Foucault helped me understand that semantics and linguistics helped shaped how knowledge was created in the production of knowledge. It was Derrida who developed theories of the relationship that linked knowledge and power as inseparable and extremely crucial to each other.

It was after History 300, Historiography, that I came to some important realizations. First, knowledge and power created each other and were locked in a dependent relationship with each other. The second was that semantics and language influenced the production of knowledge; therefore those who controlled the ability to manipulate language had the ability to alter knowledge and with that wielded power in society. Once knowledge is brought down to the masses, culture is produced and shaped. Therefore those who had the ability to produce knowledge had the ability to influence culture. Counter culture was created as anti-thesis to culture by those who disagreed with mainstream culture. Knowledge was spread to educators and then to the students. Since the knowledge produced for public education is inherently flawed, the knowledge passed to teachers is flawed. Therefore the entire public education system is flawed. While I can still say a few bad teachers can screw up a child's ability, I feel the issue lies in the education system itself. My conclusion is that society is full of imbeciles because of the knowledge and education they received from their youth. However I saw hope in the anti-thesis when I studied the civil rights movements of the 1960s in the US.

I realized that ideas originally started as counter cultures remained under constant scrutiny until society accepted them and they became a part of the mainstream. I decided the only way to produce change was to take action and not just be cynical and watch the world fall apart. As a member, project leader, and intern for NYPIRG (the New York Public Interest Research Group) I'm doing what I believe in: taking a stand and making a change. While I still retain a lot of my cynical views, I still believe in taking a stand to make a push for change. In the future I can only hope my cynicism to be proven wrong and I will see a different society where people do change.

And as for CSI and CUNY . . .

There is something I find great about CSI and the education I received on the campus, but I do believe the education prior to it needs to be reshaped and improved. However an education in my eyes is one of the most important components of a literate democratic society, and is crucial to its function. While I cannot say I hold the solutions (it would too arrogant and pompous of me to do so), I do know things need to change so that society, culture, and our way of life will improve. This understanding is the pinnacle of what constitutes the educated individual I think I have come to be.

CUNY provides a great education to more and more people who otherwise would not have it accessible. CUNY is comprised of many schools, many choices, and unlimited possibilities of learning. My only criticism lies in the lack of mandatory internships or study abroad. These experiences would enhance a student's education. However the biggest threats to CUNY lies in CUNY Pathways which intends to "dumb down" the educational experience by cutting credit requirements, adding useless pre-major classes, and getting rid of certain course requirements that create a better rounded student. The other threat lies in CUNY 20/20 which increases tuition every semester until 2016 making college less accessible to students who can barely afford to go to CUNY schools as it is. As a member of NYPIRG I hope to help defeat these threats and keep college accessible to all who want it.

M.A.

MICHAEL'S CLASSMATES RESPOND:

There are many things I have in common with Michael Abramovich. The one that heads the list is his anger and disillusionment with society and the human race altogether so that no matter where he goes, or what he does in life, the world is filled with evil bastards, or ignorant uncaring morons. I thought coming back to the College of Staten Island would be an oasis of truth and learning for me. What I have learned is that a teacher can lie about the grade he gives me, and the History department leaders will back him up.

I was a victim of bullying in Junior High School. Getting involved with my job's Labor Union was one way of fighting back, and I enjoyed it. Lately, I feel bullied by the History Department leaders. I myself had a love-hate relationship with the military. L.B.J. lied about Vietnam, so why shouldn't George Bush lie about invading Iraq? What else is new? I agree with Michael that "Knowledge is Power." Language manipulates the dissemination of knowledge to influence culture, and to keep the powerful in control.

My one problem with Michael is his grammar and sentence structure. It has too many twisted sentences, making it difficult to understand. I am far from, perfect myself. I apologize if I just appeared to be one of those "pompous imbeciles" we both despise.

It is obvious that Michael has had a less than ideal educational experience, to say the least. His negativity toward anything that is idealistic is a theme that runs throughout his essay. Michael holds all his education, prior to CSI, in utter contempt, with the exception of JROTC and his enlistment, although he is still critical of the bulk of that experience. It strikes me, that with such a pessimistic opinion of the human-race, Michael has nevertheless found himself in a personally rewarding endeavor, not to mention helping to fight the perceived injustices in society, with his work at N.Y.P.I.R.G. For all his "Nietzsche-like" prophesies and cynical attitudes Mike has seen fit to fight injustices and make life better through his work.

You have definitely been through a lot but I can't help but notice you and Henry Adams have a lot in common. Your paper does display some cynicism and although I agree with many things you say, I still believe in the human race. Terence brings up a valid point when he refers to your having a pessimistic opinion of the human race yet you joined the military to fight injustices.

Being bullied is the hardest thing for young students to endure. Luckily you were able to find an outlet that helped you stick up for yourself, because most people don't find that reprieve until college.

It is clear from reading your life story in terms of your education that your struggles have made you the strong individual you have become, mentally and physically.

Michael's educational experience is extraordinary. He joined the military after 9-11. He is courageous and though he says he was "The Outsider" many times in his life, Michael was able to learn a lot of life lessons being "The Outsider." He sees flaws within his generation because of the flawed educational system. Michael has some really good points about the educational system. I agree with some of his statements because he is not sugar coating anything. He is speaking about the educational system the way he sees it.

CHAPTER 2:

FREDERIC BEACHAM

It has come to my attention that Frederic C. Beacham III has to write an autobiographical essay for his Historical Research seminar. I anticipate much anxiety and trepidation as he attempts to write things of such a personal nature. On the other hand, it could be some sort of therapy and release from things that have been stewing inside the heart of his emotions. Many individuals with many variegated and unique personalities have affected and guided his life, for better or worse. It is difficult to evaluate and delineate what he should write about to determine who had the most influence on the development of his personality, and how they helped determine his thought processes and the manifestation of his behavior.

It appears to be transparently clear that the most influential person in Frederic Beacham's life was his father. It is true that he received the most love from his mother, and he loves her more than anything else in the world, but she did not influence his life to the extent of his father. More than anything it was the hostile, nihilistic, alienating environment his father created for him at home while he attempted to finish college. The act of being thrown out on the street, literally after finishing more than one hundred credits of college by 1974, was the most transformative experience in Frederic Beacham's life. His entire life direction and path proceed and emanate from that pivotal point in his life. The reason this juncture in his life is of paramount importance is he always asks himself what he could have become, what his life would have evolved into, if his father had allowed him to finish his Bachelor's Degree in the 1970s. A potential answer would be to examine his sister's children. Her son Joseph was encouraged to finish college and indeed to follow his dream. He not only finished college, but went to Harvard Law School and is now a lawyer with the Treasury Department in Washington D.C., with a wife and child.

As Henry Adams would say, what kind of "education" did Frederic Beacham acquire during his life? What kind of "world view" did he develop? Like Henry Adams, I believe Frederic Beacham acquired just enough understanding of how people function in their behavior, habits, and philosophical thoughts to understand the human species to the extent that he could co-habitate according to the norms of the society in which he lives. Like Henry Adams, he developed a cynical world-weariness in which his search for "education," or in more practical terms, a worthwhile meaningful existence in life, seems for all intents and purposes to have been for nothing, in that it has achieved no relevancy or legitimacy in either of their lives.

For what Henry Adams and Frederic Beacham were searching for their entire lives was not "education." No, they were and are still searching for wisdom, because education is just not about knowledge, about accumulating facts. It is what that knowledge means to you. It is only when that meaning develops a higher power beyond just the facts that knowledge becomes relevant to one's life. That relevancy is wisdom, which is designed to make your life happier and more satisfying.

There is an old saying, that "Knowledge is Power," which certainly can be true but it doesn't mean it's going to bring you a happy life. Wisdom can help you understand yourself and the world in which you live, and therefore create more harmony and satisfaction in your life. In Henry Adam's case, as well as Frederic Beacham's, they are continually searching for happiness and relevance in their lives. Their perpetual and peripatetic searching for knowledge to become "educated" has not bestowed upon them the wisdom to make themselves at peace with the world. All their educational searching for world knowledge has not resulted in peaceful self-satisfaction.

Both Henry Adams and Frederic Beacham acquired enough knowledge to find a job and eventually a career to acquire the respectability that accrues with financial security. So people like Henry Adams and Frederic Beacham, in spite of their material accomplishments of educational degrees, financial security, and service to their country will always keep searching for the true meaning of life, which is not the education one acquires from factual knowledge, but the education one acquires from the wisdom of knowing what makes you happy and contented in life on earth. Therefore, Frederic Beacham's next career path is to search for an "education" that will anoint him with wisdom.

One last thought for those who think the aforementioned written pages are demonstrative of the keen perceptibility of Frederic Beacham's insightfulness, in spite of his protestations. It is one thing to have the insight of survival skills. It is quite another to develop the wisdom of life's satisfaction.

Although one might say Frederic Beacham doth protest too loudly of his ignorance, it would be apropos to comment that he is still looking for the answers to life's questions.
F.B.

THE STORY OF BUNGALOW BILL

It all started easily enough. I was born in a hospital on Kings Highway in Brooklyn New York in 1951. My first recollection, of which I only have the vaguest of memory, was the day I ran away from home at age 3. Twenty years later, my mother reminded me of that fact in a very nurturing and supportive sort of way. I had announced to my mother, after she scolded me for something I had done in our apartment in the Gravesend section of Brooklyn, that I was going to leave the apartment to seek adventure in the world. I walked out of the apartment house and ran onto the street pavement, running down the block. I had run down one full block, stopped not knowing where I was going to next, when my mother caught up to me, grabbed my hand, and escorted me back to our apartment.

When he was twice my age, Henry Adams had exactly the opposite experience. He did not attempt to run away from home. Indeed, he did everything he could to stop from having to leave home, in this case, for the purpose of going to school. He situated himself on the stairwell, believing for all practical purposes that his pants were glued to the stairs. He had, with this attitude of confidence, convinced himself that his mother could not enforce obedience to her will upon him. Henry was completely caught off guard when his grandfather came down the stairs, took his hand, and escorted him outside the house, moving in the direction of the dreaded school house. Henry explained he did not attempt to escape Grandpa's clutches because he did not think the old gentleman was capable of walking the one mile distance to the school room itself. Upon arrival at the schoolhouse, a crestfallen Henry had to admit defeat.

I shared Henry's sense of bewilderment, with this intrusion of adult parental authority on my first taste of worldly independence. Similar to Henry, in hindsight, after we both had gotten older, we felt relief that our act of defiance was nothing more than a whiff of insouciance. We needed the love and nurturing of our parents more than anything else. This was a reminder that we needed to be cared for.

I believe this early childhood incident serves as a metaphor for what happens in general to all people going out into the world to discover what place on this earth one belongs to, whether it be spiritual, emotional, or geographical. One could broach the opinion that I have been running, figuratively speaking on the run, searching for life's meaning ever since that Spring day in 1954.

My worldview and any physical worldly surroundings were bound to expand anyway, unbeknownst to me, when my parents bought a detached house in the Marine Park section of Brooklyn in the fall of 1954. Now, I could run around without having to run away! I became pre-occupied with making mud pies and digging holes in the ground, filling toy dump trucks up with dirt and transporting that dirt to another section of our new backyard to make more mud pies. Tearing up the backyard was exhausting work. It required all my attention during the warmer months of the year, until the snow fell in late December. In the 1950's and 1960's in New York City, we had a lot more snow than we have now.

When I was past the age of three I noticed a little baby had come along, but I couldn't play with her because she needed the special attention all new born babies require from their mother. My life of homebound activity was about to come to an end. Although a two story house plus a dirt backyard to ruin our clothes had more than enough space to exhaust the energy of a five year old, it was my only world. At age five, I entered kindergarten and suddenly I was in this tremendous building, five stories instead of two with vastly more space than a house. I was afraid and intimidated, and cried the first few days at school. My mother took me the first two weeks, until I got comfortable and confident in my surroundings. I remember a Mrs. DeGroot who was a teacher and a friend of my mother who let me know I was being watched over and cared for. It helped build my confidence. In the 1950's and early 1960's, most elementary school teachers were female. It was around 1958 and I was in first grade, when I came to school, and almost all the teachers, which meant every adult female in the school, were crying! I gathered up all my nerve, and went up to one of the few male teachers, and asked him, "Why are they crying?" He told me, "Errol Flynn died." I pretended I knew what he was talking to me about, thanked him, and walked away.

When it came to ethnic, racial, or religious identity, I did not feel different from other kids my age. It was a white, working class neighborhood. Amazingly, so it still is today. It was and still is a very enclosed insular neighborhood. The elementary school, P.S. 207, was four blocks away so I walked to school. My church, Holy Trinity Lutheran church, was only six blocks away. The Catholic kids went to Saint Thomas Aquinas. Nobody ever discussed religion. None of us cared about it much. In the sixth grade, I got my first inkling of ethnic consciousness. We had to give a presentation of our ethnic background in front of the class, explaining where our ancestors came from. My mother gave me information concerning the history of my Great Grandfather who came from Germany. There were rumblings from the Jewish kids about my German ancestry on my mother's side. I did not know they were annoyed. I would find out two years later in Junior High School 278 when I took Social Studies, and began to learn about world history. I felt unfortunate for what it brought upon myself. I liked the Jewish kids because the boys always had something to say, unlike the Italians who were quieter, and the Jewish girls were sexy, although I knew nothing about sex appeal or the birds and the bees, at age 12. Remember, this is 1963-1964.

It was at this juncture that I became enamored with the city of New York public education system. By the age of 13, with the increasing maturation and developmental skills of a growing adolescent brain, for me Junior High School became a stepping stone whose successful completion led to high school, which was nothing less than a college preparatory institution. Everything in Junior High School seemed to point to the beginning of an ascent into adulthood, and the gradual weaning away of childhood. The girls began to blossom and physically develop, which made the boys take notice, whether they wanted to or not. We all began to build specific interests according to the individual predilections of our personality. The music teacher, Mr. Ernest Nichols, told me to speak louder one day. He kept on saying "Louder, Louder!" I didn't know he was testing my voice. He then informed me I was in the school chorus. When I protested to my father, looking for parental support, he took the side of the teacher and said I should try to see if I would like it. I still can remember some of the songs we used to sing. It started a lifelong appreciation of music, including everything from classical to rock and roll.

During Junior High School there occurred my first traumatic experience in life. My father was a public school teacher, teaching in ghetto schools in Brooklyn. He contracted tuberculosis from poor students who could not afford to pay for medical care to prevent illness and disease. My father was sent to Kings County Medical Center where he lived for a year to recuperate. My mother had to go back to work full-time to support the family. In 1964 I saw my father just three times. His three children had to do a lot more chores around the house that their mother had once done. This was the time that I started to stutter, and develop a nervousness which persisted into adulthood.

By the time I entered ninth grade, my father was back home and everything was back to normal. I enjoyed singing in school chorus. This extra-curricular activity made me feel important because it allowed me to socialize with the more intelligent, academically proficient students. This gave me confidence that I would fit into an academic program when I entered high school in the tenth grade. I continued with chorus in high school, but it wasn't as much fun as Junior High, so I dropped that after my sophomore year. I also had too much schoolwork to continue. However, I couldn't resist staying involved socially, so I joined my Hi-Y Church basketball team at Flatlands Dutch Reformed church on Kings Highway.

I enjoyed myself growing up in Brooklyn. Between my friends and school, I had a balanced network of socialization in which I participated. A pattern of human development was emerging. As I progressed in life, the world in which I lived and the environment I inhabited expanded continuously. At first, this could be attributed to my brain and body physically growing. What is interesting, after my brain and bodily growth ceased in my chronological twenties, I continued to pursue the means and methods of acquiring new knowledge, both as an everyday life experiential situation, and in an academic environment.

The question should be asked, what is educational? It is my personal life experience, that you acquire education wherever you find it. To me, educational initiatives encourage all learning, which enables us to improve the quality and livability of our life. It has been difficult for me to separate the interpersonal sociological skills I acquired by functioning in the real world of everyday life from the strict confines of formal academic school ing. You could say that the rules of formal academia are much more rigidly defined than the psychological interaction of everyday life. In school, one follows rules concerning study habits established by the teacher to conform to assigned reading, test and term papers. However, there are also the rules of life, or societal norms, which I came to develop as well during my educational journey. After I left college at age twenty-three, without having received my Bachelor's degree I went to work for the city of New York, staying for thirty-three years. The main benefits I received from my employment, besides getting a paycheck once every two weeks, and eventually a pension, was the knowledge I acquired in how to relate to people, how to function in a work-related environment in which the employees have to develop behavioral skills to negotiate their personal conduct with their fellow employees. Although I took psychology classes at Richmond College that defined and analyzed human behavior, it takes quite another category of criteria to coexist with other employees in a place of employment. This is an educational experience that teaches "people skills." This is what formal academic, or school environment cannot teach.

This is why I say it is impossible to discuss one's educational experience in terms of strict academics. I will give you an unfortunate recent example. Last term I took History 300. The coursework was very difficult. The readings were convoluted, confusing, and contradictory. I do admit though, that I learned an awful lot, but only because I studied very hard. The level of difficulty of the course material was only half the problem. What made it doubly worse was the teacher's inability to communicate his knowledge of the course material to students. One of the most common problems, and a most egregious one in my opinion of college academia, is to hire brilliant scholars based solely on their knowledge of their field of expertise. This teacher, who is not teaching at the College of Staten Island for the spring 2012 semester, knew his subject matter, and his mastery of it was apparent. His one major professional flaw was that he could not delineate and distill the information he was trying to impart in a language that could be understood and recognized by his students. His communication skills as a teacher were deplorable.

What became worse was his inability to treat his students like human beings. This is difficult to explain. He acted very robotic and insensitive. Clearly this was a product of his childhood development and familial development, as is true with so much else in life for everyone. The proof was in the pudding. As the semester progressed, more and more students dropped out of his class. I honestly believe the students were afraid of him. He took offense at any opinion which put into question his teaching. One essay I submitted on Voltaire I thought was brilliant, and believed I would certainly get an "A". He said he would not grade it as submitted because I used too many big words which he could not comprehend in the text of the essay. I got angry and asked him if he wanted me to "dumb down" the content of the essay. I can't recall having this kind of fear and loathing for a teacher except one other time in high school. I felt traumatized from the experience. I do admit that going on vacation the third week in January to the Caribbean did help to settle my frazzled nerves.

Education therefore isn't just some theoretical understanding of abstract academic concepts of the sciences, or social sciences, but also the product of communicative skills that can be interpreted in common everyday language. The education of school must therefore interact with the education of the "streets smarts" commonsense of everyday life. However, as my aforementioned teacher so aptly demonstrated, having only one educational skillset without the other can be harmful to one's career or personal life.

This brings me to the polar opposite case study, that of my fellow employees at the New York City Transit Authority. They were totally street smart and always knew which way the wind was blowing, but 90% of them barely graduated from high school. They would have known which way the wind was blowing, but they didn't know why it was blowing in the first place. I did know because I was intellectually curious. I read The New York Times every day. I understood history, politics, and popular culture on a level of comprehension that they couldn't approach.

After being employed by the New York City Transit Authority for five years, I had once again the yearning for adventure and, like Henry Adams, a desire to expand my educational horizons. I went into basic training with the Air Force in October of 1984. I was also on active duty for tech school and on-the-job training until April of 1985. Thereafter, I was an active duty for one weekend a month, and two weeks a year until 1990. I entered the military for other reasons than just adventure. I felt guilty about not having served in the Vietnam War. I had gone straight from high school to college in the early 1970's. Another reason I joined was I admired the life of David Niven, the British actor.

In the 1970's, I had read his autobiography, *The Moon's a Balloon*. He had graduated from college, Britain's Sandhurst Academy. A few years later, after tiring of army life, he went to Hollywood. When World War II started, he went back home to England to volunteer for military service.

He commanded British Special Forces raids inside German occupied territory in Europe, cheating death many times. He wasn't just a charming, handsome actor with an English accent playing fighter pilots in movies such as World War One's 1938 movie, "Dawn Patrol". He was the real deal. He had walked the walk. I wanted to do the same thing. In spite of Henry Adams's portrayal of himself as a "Laurel and Hardy" bumbling ignoramus searching futilely for educational wisdom, he was a talented, knowledgeable foreign policy advisor to the United States government for many decades. Like David Niven, I had a love-hate affair with the military. I was proud of my service, but I did not like the bureaucracy.

I got involved in politics at my job in the transit system and became a Labor Union activist. I did volunteer work for the Transit Authority Labor Union to fight any politicians on a borough, city, or national level who wanted to ruin our employee benefits. Our union gave campaign support to those who wanted to preserve or enhance them. I truly believed then, and now, that our cause is honorable and just, because the political and managerial elite have all the power and money, and the average working person is financially marginalized. Our biggest victory was getting David Dinkins elected mayor in 1989. Our biggest defeat was Eric Vetaliano losing a congressional contest to Vito Vosella in 1997. My target in 2012 is to get rid of Michael Grimm. My reward for years of political activism was attending Bill Clinton's inauguration in 1997. It was my role to help educate the street smart but educationally functional illiterates on my job. It was not easy. At first they thought I was some oddball space cadet when I discussed issues of labor history. Slowly but surely they came to realize I had my facts straight, and I was on their side.

Where did I come to comprehend, and what's more important, acquire a desire for learning in general, and a penchant for political and historical analysis in particular? It was the two year Associate in Science degree I got from Staten Island community college and my junior year as a History major at Richmond College. The most interesting course I ever took was Michael Greenberg's American Colonial History. An interest in this nation's early history continues to persist to this day. Sandi Cooper's

Twentieth Century Europe gave me an understanding of European political forces which helped shape the national identity of late twentieth century America. The charmingly dry mid-western wit of Roger Moorhus came through in his Early Modern Germany course, which included an examination of another rebel, Martin Luther. I was enthralled by the European charm of Alice Shuster in History 100, and secretly had the hots for her. It would be an understatement to say the college courses I took piqued my intellectual curiosity, just as I refused to "dumb down" to last term's subtle intimidation by my professor. College taught me to not "dumb down" to my bosses with the New York City Transit Authority even though I showed them the utmost respect. They especially did not like it when I wouldn't "dumb down" when it came to making them comply with labor union regulations.

In the final analysis of all of my life's varied stages and aspects, my college courses trained me to think critically. They demanded that I write term papers in which the supposition of my thematic object of analysis is supported with the facts, and nothing but the facts.

This desire for knowledge, learning, and academic achievement is what drove me back to the College of Staten Island to finish my senior year, after having dropped out of school in 1975. This desire to return to college was tantamount to an obsession, which was fueled by tremendous anger and hatred for having been forcibly expelled from college by my father. For most of the thirty-one years I worked for the Transit Authority, I psychologically suppressed the yearning I had to finish my college degree. I sublimated my educational ambitions by becoming a workaholic. I refused to work just a regular 8 hour shift. I worked as much overtime as I could get, for as long as I could get it, for 31 years. My free time, what little that I had, was dedicated to labor union politics. In between all of this, I was able to fall in love a number of times, but I was too hyperactive in my life to stop and smell the roses with one of the many wonderful women with whom I was in love.

All I knew at the time was my father was an evil sadist for forcibly evicting me from his house, knowing I couldn't continue to go to college once I was a bum on the streets. Many decades later, I discovered the reason he did not want me to finish my college education. It was the jealousy he felt that I was going to school full-time, and not having to work. What is of paramount importance is this; thanks to the diabolical machinations of my father, he forcibly led me into the exact same educational experiences that he was compulsively coerced into following himself. My father's father, Grandpa Beacham, forced his son in the early 1930's to drop out of high school during the Great Depression to help feed the family. My father went to night school to finish high school.

Like myself decades later, my father, desperate for a job, took every civil service test that he could, and became a fireman. He hated the Fire Department but thanks to work assignments called "mutuals" on his job, went to Brooklyn College part-time, and got his degree. After twenty years, he retired from the Fire Department and became a New York City Public School teacher. Lifelong learning in general and pursuing numerous master's degrees in particular, became my father's lifelong obsession. The reason is obvious. The anger he felt for his father for forcing him to go to work at age fifteen.

My father (Ha, Ha!) was despicable enough to wait until I had finished my junior year of college to play the same dirty trick on me. Like my father, my anger and hatred motivated me to want to be a success in life. I did not want to be a failure. I did not want to be poor. I had the traumatic experience of living in welfare rooming houses and collecting food stamps. I went from middle class respectability to poverty very quickly. I became fearful I could never support a family. I will never acquire three Master's degrees the way he did. I would be happy to settle for one, along with a wife and a child.

Like my father, being deprived and denied the education we both valued was a major motivating factor in making me strive and achieve a modicum of success in life.

At the very end of the book, in the chapter "*Nunc Age*," Henry Adams's closest friend John Hay dies. Adams just doesn't mourn Hay, he seems to think this has also presaged the foretelling of his own death: "It was only the quiet summons to follow, the assent to dismissal. It was time to go. The three friends had begun life together; and the last of the three had no motive, no attraction, to carry it on after the others had gone. Education had ended for all three."

I know how Henry Adams felt, because I feel the same way. My mother is in a nursing home in Staten Island due to dementia. It is getting worse every week. She will probably die in the nursing home. I sympathize with Henry Adams's experience of deep despair especially knowing he was getting older himself. The sense of loss is horrible.

However, in terms of a learning experience which encompassed a lifetime of educational human development, everyone should be as fortunate to live the chronologically long life as Henry Adams did, with most of it occurring in a state of abundantly beneficent health, in pursuit of his Education.

And as for CSI and CUNY

I started my college education in the fall of 1969 at the Staten Island Community College campus as an engineering major. I was always fascinated with how things were structured, whether buildings or microscopic particles. In 1972 I received my Associate in Science Community College degree. After that I went to Kansas State University to look for Middle America and finish my engineering degree. However, I had lost interest in analyzing science problems, and so I escaped into a History and Politics major. The out-of-state tuition at Kansas State University was prohibitive, so I came back to New York City to pursue my studies in History at Richmond College, the upper level division of CUNY in Staten Island.

After finishing my junior year there, I made the Dean's list under the Honor-Pass-Fail grading system. At this point, my parents decided I was an annoyance spending my life going to school and studying, even though my father was a teacher. I was forced to drop out of school and leave home. After a couple years of struggle, I wound up working for the New York City Transit Authority.

I did not feel like a typical blue collar worker because I did not think like one. I felt that my coworkers were too prone to taking the easy way out when it came to analyzing life situations, dismissing the vicissitudes of life with phrases such as "it was fate" and "oh well, what are you going to do?" Three years of college had taught me to not rationalize life's circumstances as the inevitability of fate, but to analyze each situation as I did to answer test questions, to understand what could be done to solve the conundrum of each situation. I put these educational skills to good use in solving work related problems after obtaining a supervisory level position.

It was therefore with high hopes that I could put these analytical skills back to work once again in an educational format after I retired from my career as a civil servant. I did well after returning to college, getting a B+ in Chinese History, and then an A in Historical Methods. Then I took History 300 with Professor "Sweetheart" and all hell broke loose. I put the answers to part B of the first examination on the answer sheet, instead of the test booklet, and he wouldn't evaluate part B for grading purposes, and failed me, although the average test score was 53 for that exam. He didn't like an essay I wrote on Voltaire because I used too many "complicated" words.

When I received a grade of B-, I filed an appeal with the history department chairman. The appeals committee found my grade appeal was without any merit. They did not give an explanation as to why they rejected my appeal, and they said I could go no further in attempting to appeal my grade. What boggles the mind is Sweetheart couldn't even correctly add the calculation of his dysfunctional grading system. He said I got an 81 average. However, using his own grade figures, my average final grade is 83.4, which is more than a B minus. This means those four tenured, PhD professors on the committee refused to admit Swihart couldn't add one-plus-one, using his own figures.

I had a tremendous amount of evidence to win my grade appeal. The refusal of the powers that be in the History department to acknowledge that evidence as legitimate caused me to become very angry and disillusioned with the quality of the teaching staff in the History department. What they did to me is cruel and mean-spirited. I have completely lost respect for the History department, and the College of Staten Island. I had come back to college with idealistic aspirations of accomplishing a life-long achievement. One way or another, I will eventually leave the College of Staten Island with a feeling of resignation, even failure.

There is one thing I do know. I did darn good work in Sweetheart's class, getting very good grades, except for the happenstance of the first test. I was one of the smartest students in the class. Up until now, I worked very hard to do excellent work. For the department committee who would not recognize my above average efforts, they can go to hell.

I've learned the futility of attempting to achieve remedial redress from the establishment power structure at the College of Staten Island. The grade appeal process is blatantly skewed in favor of the institution. It leaves me with a feeling of powerlessness and helplessness.

I attended the Middle States Accreditation for the College of Staten Island, on Tuesday, April 3, 2012, at the college. Every single one of the students who spoke in the auditorium, uniformly, unanimously, gave their laudatory approval about how wonderful their college educational experiences had been. That is, until I spoke about my experiences with History 300 about the patent callousness of Mr. Sweetheart's approach to teaching, the fact that he could not even add my grade components up correctly leaving me with a lower final mark, the arrogant denial of the department committee, who are allowed to escape total responsibility for their actions by not even being required to justify their behavior with a valid explanation of their actions. Everything is just perfect in the Land of Oz, or at least that is what you were led to believe at the Middle States Accreditation coronation. The college is infallible. Therefore, any student's grade appeal will always be denied.

This is tough. Very tough. Since I have written my College of Staten Island student life experiences within the textual confines of The Education of Henry Adams during the spring of 2012, a lot of "educating" has occurred in the life of Frederic Beacham. When I gave the title of my autobiographical segment "The Continuing Story of Bungalow Bill," it was a sarcastic, farcical criticism of my entire life. The farcical nature of my segment's title has everything to do with Henry Adams's Education. There is an old saying that you develop wisdom as you get older. At age 61, I am within a few years of Henry Adams' age when he wrote "The Education." What we seem to have in common is an intrinsic, almost pathological fear that the more you know, the more you realize that you know very little. Not just about a formal academic education, but even much more regrettably, the education of learning about life itself.

That song sung by Dionne Warwick in the mid-1960s, "What's It All about Alfie," from the movie, "Alfie," starring a young Michael Caine, could have instead been the title for Henry Adams' book. For Henry Adams, like myself, seems to go through life, and live his life according to the career path and life style he has decided upon, whether it was to his specifications or not, without understanding the true meaning of life. This means enjoying life itself, and feeling happy. That every day brings a new experience, and a renewed sense of being. Real wisdom is knowing what you want to do with your life when you are young, and you then proceed to fulfill the goals of those dreamlike aspirations.

Wisdom is not what myself and Henry Adams have experienced, which is to comprehend when you are older that all the knowledge, or "education" in the world is not what is important or relevant to the applicability to being successful in life. The question is: Did you create life experiences that you were happy living? There is an exasperation in the tone of Henry Adams' book, especially at the end, on the last page when he mourns the death of his three closest friends, and foreshadows his own impending death.

My mother is dying of Alzheimer's disease in Clove Lakes Nursing Home. I doubt if she will live beyond February, 2013. There is a mournful regret that I did not spend more time experiencing my parents' company. I rarely experienced my father's social embrace, or personal empathy after he forced me out of his house following my junior year at Richmond College in 1974. I've spent most of my life trying to prove my father wrong, by attempting to become a success, working long overtime hours on my job making money. Then also by participating in political volunteerism to fill my life.

In the end, however, all that whirlwind of human activity, like the locomotion of Henry Adams' Anglophile, Eurocentric diplomatic Foreign Service career seems to come crashing down on him in the end. On page 396 of The Education, he states: "It was not even the suddenness of the shock, or the sense of void, that threw Adams into the depths of Hamlet's Shakespearean silence in the full flare of Paris frivolity in its favorite haunt, where worldly vanity reached its most futile climax in human history; it was only the quiet summons to follow, -the assent to dismissal. It was time to go. The three friends had begun life together; and the last of the three had no motive - no attraction - to carry it on after the others had gone. Education had ended for all three, and only beyond some remoter horizon could its values be fixed or renewed."

It seems like a depressing black hole Henry Adams has fallen into, something relative to how I feel with the impending death of my mother. Like Henry Adams, I never married or had children, although I had always wanted to do so. Unless I am misinterpreting Henry Adams, he would prefer, if it was only possible, like myself, a life do-over. Instead of being an observer of life, of its Education, he, like myself, would be much happier to just experience the spontaneity and movement of life's interpersonal interaction itself. To experience the joy of the act of living itself.

In retrospect, maybe I should not have gone back to college after I retired from my job in the year 2011. In reaction to my father mistreating me, I still felt motivated to do the right thing in my life, so I could be a success. For thirty years, that had meant going back to college to finish my bachelor's degree, after I had started to collect my pension. As it turns out in hindsight, returning to college was anti-climactic, because I did not experience a long-lost sense of accomplishment because it was after-the-fact. I no longer needed a college degree to develop a career. I had just finished working for the City of New York for thirty-three years. However, like my father, I always had a thirst for knowledge and learning, and so, like him, I was going to college well into middle age.

My mother was very proud of me when I went back to college. She knew it had been my life-long dream. When she broke her left leg in December of 2011, my family thought it would be a temporary situation. I started History 400 in January 2012 with that mindset. After surgery, the recovery period in the Nursing Home allowed her dementia to get much worse due to her immobility. As a result of what happened to my mother, I didn't know if I would have the mental fortitude to continue in my studies with the college in the year 2012 due to feelings of loneliness and emotional abandonment. Of course financially, I am much more level-headed and adroit. I had substituted emotional well-being for fiscal diligence a long time ago. My mother had promised me time and time again a big party to celebrate my graduation from the College of Staten Island. She will have left this earthly life by the time

I march down the aisle on graduation day. I don't know how I will be able to do it. I know I will cry. How do you start your life all over again after you have passed your sixtieth birthday?

Scientists now know what causes dementia and Alzheimer's disease. There will be a cure within five to ten years. My mind feels young and nimble, ready to conquer life's next big challenges, but I cannot do it by myself intellectually or emotionally. Like Henry Adams, I would like to dispense with the cognitive formalities of life which dictate one must obey the requisites of the societal constructs of professional careerism, collegiate academics, or the mannerisms of formal etiquette. He, as well as myself, would much rather promulgate predilections of the propensities of that behavioral human choice which makes us enjoy our life experience, in which we make interpersonal dialogue with family, friends and neighbors. Otherwise, we become an atrophied, dysfunctional, socially alienated species. If not to do so, then Pink Floyd warns us with this admonition, "Hey, teacher, leave those kids alone. All in all, you're just a brick in the wall."

Ten days after I wrote the above addendum, my mother, Doris Ebert Beacham, died of Alzheimer's disease at Clove Lakes Nursing Home in Staten Island, on February 18, 2013. My loss feels like a bottomless pit, a black hole which is difficult to escape from. I never thought of myself as a "momma's boy". I have been financially independent from my parents since I was twenty-three. However, no matter how independent I was of my parents, after my father's death in 1990, I always felt I could bounce life's issues off my mother, and talk to her about any of life's situations I was involved in, and seek her wise paternalistic advice. It doesn't matter that I have two lovely sisters. It's a completely different mindset. I am seeking psychological counsel to deal with this crisis in my life, but the loneliness and aloneness seems many times unbearable. I realize now I am doing everything thirty years too late. This includes graduating from college, and of most important significance, the desire to marry and have children.

I don't know where this "education" will all lead to, and where it will all end besides death, of course. Then again, neither did Henry Adams.

I have to seek to accomplish realistic goals and pursue achievable accomplishments that will make my life one of happiness, and peaceful fulfillment. The question is this: Is it already too late? Having already spent most of my life struggling to survive, and achieve a modicum of financial success. The answer is: Don't put off life's happiness and satisfaction too long or else you would have already lived your life, and life would have passed you by. I am optimistic that it is not too late for me.

At risk of belaboring the point, it should also be noted that my mother died on the same day that her father was born, as well as the same day that her granddaughter, my sister's daughter, was born. Also, it now occurs to me that if I had waited a year to go back to school, my mother would have by then broken her leg, and been in the nursing home. I would have been in a too distraught mental state to return to school and concentrate on studying. In retrospect, it was tough enough concentrating on History 400 in the spring of 2012! I had been feeling very stressed out after retiring from my job after 33 years. Something, however, inside of me felt compelled, some psychic force, urged me to carry on, and go back to college in the fall semester of 2010, even while still working! As I said before, my mother told me numerous times that she was proud of me for finally returning to school, and for the good grades I was mostly receiving! She, however, won't be there.

Today, March 1, 2013, I submitted these additions to Maria in the History department. O.K., welcome to Sequester. Who cares if we don't get our paychecks from the City of New York!! There's always food stamps. Oh, I'm sorry, that Federal government program was just sequestered out of business!

More seriously, one last thought. This past Monday or Tuesday night, I woke up at four in the morning in panic, thinking of my mother. In my

bedroom, I saw an orange mist, but at first I did not realize it as such. Then through the mist I saw a white cross for a few seconds. After about twenty seconds the room became clear, after the mist had slowly dissipated. That is when I realized there had been a mist. I did not imagine this. It really happened. Although not a Catholic, as a Protestant my mother believed in Jesus, and an afterlife in Heaven, and so do I.
F.B.

FREDERICK'S CLASSMATES RESPOND:

It has to be very tough to feel betrayed by your father and be removed from the excellent education you were receiving. Unlike most other people who are homeless, you were able to overcome that and have a successful career. Now, you're coming full circle and finishing your school education like you always dreamed of doing.

I too had the same History 300 class with Fred. I can understand his frustration with the professor and grade received at the end of the semester. However, I feel you can take a positive out of everything in life, and that class gave us an insight into what a graduate class feels like!

Fred you have come a long way and may have had some struggles you seem to always push through. Don't stress too much on history 300; you did a good job!

Your story is a fruitful one, full of many life experiences that has brought you to this point. It is clear that you have always worked hard for the betterment of yourself and that you will continue to do so as you move forward in finally receiving your college degree.

Even though you had a tough life Fred, it seems like you came up from the hardships and are starting fresh.

Dear Fred, Your story was so interesting to me, it's unfortunate the obstacles you had endured but they only gave you more ambition and determination to become such an intelligent person.

CHAPTER 3:

MATTHEW BUSH

For many people, becoming educated is a long and tedious process. They might complete all of their schooling but only retain limited knowledge, while others can use personal experiences from outside of the classroom as the basis of their education. In comparison to my mom, my experience of education differs from hers. Although I'm still a college student, I have been able to see where I have failed throughout my academic career thus far and what I was able to do to fix it. From elementary school through high school I have had different obstacles in the different schools that I had to face in order to be where I am today. My views on education changed drastically throughout the years, as well as my views of myself as a person.
M.B.

THE EDUCATION OF MATTHEW BUSH

As a child I felt like education was learning the basics of the future, and I didn't necessarily have to worry about any negative vibes at home. My mother grew up in a very poor household where it was a constant struggle and a poor environment in general. She moved out of the house at 18, and most of her education came from her childhood experiences. As she got older, she decided that she wanted to work in the New York court system. Originally she had aspired to be a lawyer until she became more aware of the exceptionally long work hours that the job required. Instead she opted to become a court reporter, where the hours were much more predictable. The salary was also sufficient for what she was looking for, and so it became her career. She has been able to overcome her background to be become a successful, very well educated person today.

My formal education began when I began elementary school at the age of 4, which is also the time of the first learning experiences I can remember. I attended elementary school at P.S.32, and from kindergarten through fifth grade I was routinely one of the top students in my class. Throughout this period, I realize that some of my success can be attributed to my mother who was continuously stressing the importance of school to me and my two brothers. Homework was assigned daily, but it was always just a few assignments that could be completed in a short amount of time. Tests were assigned on certain days of the week so I was always prepared for them.

School was new to me and I had high aspirations. At such a young age, one believes that anything is possible. I had thoughts of becoming anything from the president to a lawyer, but deep down my dream was to become a teacher. This desire contributed to my strong grades, so much as to where I was devastated when I was not selected for the accelerated program when it was first offered entering fourth grade. I have always been a social person, and unfortunately this was the reason for my being shut out of the program. Looking back, I can say that my willingness to become friends with just about anybody has helped me to this day. No matter what level of the school "hierarchy" anyone was I was always able to be friendly with them. From the nerdy kids to the popular ones I was always able to fit in nicely. I would continue to excel in my grades and was eventually crowned the Spelling Bee champion in fifth grade, becoming the first non-accelerated student to win the competition in years. I would lose in the district, coming in a respectable 15th out of 50 while competing students ranged from fifth to eighth grade. Although I was very disappointed that I didn't win, the spelling bee served as a learning experience because it helped convince myself that I was an intelligent person, and that the accelerated program doesn't necessarily determine who the brightest students are. As elementary school came to a close, I graduated with most of my goals completed and I looked forward to the challenge of junior high. My anticipation was that I would continue to receive similarly high grades, but there were unforeseen obstacles that I had not previously encountered, and perhaps didn't handle in the best way possible.

Junior High school began in the year 2001 for me, and immediately I saw it was a different atmosphere than elementary school. When I first entered I.S. 24, I still took it very seriously for all of sixth grade. The whole year was essentially a transition period to a completely different way of schooling. My grades were still high, but began a steady decline as the time passed. It was around sixth grade that I received my first job as a paper boy. This was when my priorities in school began to wane. Along my paper route I came to meet several people who eventually became very good friends, often delaying me from delivering my papers. Instead I preferred to hang out, and by the time I got home it would be too late to start homework. Unlike elementary school, I didn't have someone always over my shoulder making sure that my homework was completed. Also, in junior high I had a different teacher for every class, which meant that although some teachers were very good, some were very poor at their profession. There wasn't the same emphasis on collecting homework and this made it less urgent to complete it every day, especially since there were no consequences. School became impersonal, because you had each teacher for roughly forty minutes as opposed to nearly the whole day. I remember in my math class in eighth grade the teacher had lost her grasp on the class. Every day the classroom was a battlefield in which markers, crayons, fruits, and other objects were thrown across the classroom in an attempt to hit other classmates. We never got into trouble for this, and that whole year the class never learned math.

There were more people to meet and it was a much more diverse environment. I was able to become friends with people from other neighborhoods who had different personalities from the kids I had grown up with. It was harder for me to hang out with these old friends often since I didn't have a reliable source of transportation, but it was probably for the best, being that these people were troublemakers. I remember hearing how they would throw rocks at cars and eventually got into a lot of trouble. Thankfully I was never present for that, and even if I was I definitely would not have contributed. We always got along, but it wasn't the greatest group of people to be associated with. As junior high came to a close, my grades weren't as high as elementary school, but I was still an above average student. I had acquired some bad tendencies that unfortunately transferred over into high school.

High school was similar to junior high in that it was a completely new environment, but it was also a Catholic school, which was a first for me. I had to attend school every day in uniform, as opposed to wearing whatever I wanted as in previous years. It was also an all boy school, which took a little getting used to. Much to my surprise, the discipline of the teachers varied tremendously. There were plenty of teachers who seemed to care very little about the subject they were teaching and it had a trickling effect on the students. Cheating on exams was widespread, and people often relied on this over studying.

I continued my bad habits from junior high despite the constant pestering from my parents that my grades were very important for getting into a good college. I didn't exactly listen to their advice, because as a teenager I often felt that I knew what was best. I also felt that regardless of my grades I wouldn't be rejected from any schools. My parents tried to make their message clear by sending me to summer school for a class that I had passed during the year, but the point didn't get across. When summer school began, I excelled. I finished with an average in the high 90s and felt really confident that I could continue the same work when the school year rolled around.

Instead, it was more of the usual. In summer school, with a small class and only one teacher, it was easier for me to respond. I had the same teacher the next year, and despite a strong start I once again fell to an average grade. The most common thing I heard from teachers in high school was my potential was to be very smart, but that it was up to me to put in the effort. I never held up my end of the bargain, choosing instead to play video games and hang out with my friends rather than do homework.

Even though it would break my heart to see my mom get upset, I found it extremely difficult to change my habits. I needed a wake-up call, and I received one. My parents' warning came true when I wasn't accepted into the college I had been hoping to attend, thus winding up in the College of Staten Island where I am currently enrolled.

Upon entering college, my hopes were high and a standard was set. I was accepted into the Verrazano School and I had to maintain a grade point average of 3.00 to be retained by the program. I had hoped to achieve this, but unlike high school nothing is given to you in college. I struggled a little bit, and was removed from the program at the conclusion of my third semester. This was devastating to me, and it was almost as if a switch had turned on inside my head that made me want to be better.

It took me a lot longer then I liked, but I finally realized that school was important and more than just fun and games. Professor Durando, an English professor at the college, greatly improved my writing and helped me in ways that no other teacher previously had. She gave interesting topics for assignments, was very hands on, and truly enjoyed watching her students learn. Her classes were fun and educational and I looked forward to attending her class every week. It was around then that I decided that getting average grades, or just being satisfied with a passing grade was not the way to approach my classes. From that point on, I began to take school much more seriously. I never again missed an assignment, and I put a lot more effort into my papers.

I have since completed several more semesters while greatly improving my grade point average. It's unfortunate that I couldn't realize my priorities sooner, for if I had then I most likely would have gone away to college or at the very least remained a member of the Verrazano program. After many different experiences throughout my life in different schools, it appears that I have come full circle. At times, I still revert back to my sloppy habits and become lazy, but the days of missing assignments or completely blowing them off are over.

My education contrasts with that of my mother's in that school was extremely important to her. Her upbringing differed greatly from mine due to her hard upbringing. My grandfather on my mother's side immigrated to the United States from Italy during his teenage years. When he arrived in the U.S. he faced many difficulties, like other immigrants, such as trouble speaking English, finding a decent job, and supporting the family he would eventually have. My mom is one of five children, and she was raised in a small house where she had to share her room with her three sisters. From a young age she understood that other kids in her neighborhood had it easier and they ridiculed her as a child. Her family was very poor and she was never able to have the luxuries of nice clothes, new toys, or any new fads. Instead, they shared hand-me-downs and clothes that were always a size too big or a size too small. My mother's siblings also faced similar struggles and had difficult childhoods. Her father was unable to receive a proper education because of an eyesight problem that was very difficult to deal with, coupled with the new culture of the United States. He understood the value of an education and thus drilled the importance of it into my mother's head from the day she first began school. His lessons created her personal desire not only to succeed, but to excel in school.

Since my mother had no money growing up, she was faced with the choice of either going to school and getting a low salaried job, to be supported by her future husband or to work hard and receive a job that would enable her to support herself and her future family. Her decision was to get as good a job as possible. She studied often and went above and beyond in doing her work in order to make her parents proud. She was determined to get as much out of her education as possible while realizing her dream of becoming a successful person. Teachers had taken an interest in her due to her willingness to learn, and my mom believes that they were a very large reason in her success. Along the way she was involved in several relationships before finally settling down with my dad.

One of the experiences from which my mom was able to learn was a relationship in her early twenties. She was dating a man she loved, and eventually became engaged to. It wasn't the perfect relationship though, as my mom had doubts about his future employment options. My mother was faced with the decision of whether to end the relationship, and after realizing that he was making no changes she broke off the engagement. It was a heartbreaking, gut-wrenching decision that she felt was necessary to make in order to avoid having a struggling family like the one she grew up in. She would eventually meet my father who had a stable job and who was able to help support the family that they planned to have.

Currently I am studying to become a teacher. My hope is that I can one day become a high school history teacher. My past experiences in school have made me shy away from subjects such as math, science, and English because of my struggles in those classes. Only a select few of my teachers had an interest in their class, and the ones that truly cared were the ones that I did the best with. The teachers who showed little care for how well their students performed were treated with the same attitude. My experiences with these teachers led me to studying history, which is based upon facts, since it has always interested me to see how people and environments have changed.

Thus far, I can say that I have become the person that I have envisioned as a kid. I have managed to keep relationships with my good friends and have become someone that they can confide in. I have learned from my experiences to be the person I could have become, and am happy with the results. My mother's past was very different from mine as far as education goes, but we have both been able to adapt to our situations in a positive way. Although my path differed from my mom's I know that she has been a great role model for me and despite her struggles as a child. She has made the most out of her situation and made me proud to be her son.

And as for CSI and CUNY

The CUNY system, despite its flaws, was very effective for me. I don't have many of the issues that most other students do. Once you enter college, it's more of what you make of it then what is provided for you.

The College Of Staten Island helped me in more ways than one. Although there are and will always be professors that are better than others, I learned that the classes are what I make of them. Regardless of who was teaching me, the students are responsible for doing their reading and submitting assignments. If I had trouble with a class, there was always free tutoring available to aid me. This is a great benefit because tutors outside of the school can be very expensive. There is also a library that has a vast amount of resources readily available to me. If the library doesn't have the item that I need, chances are one of the other CUNY schools do and I can pick up the book with no hassle.

The College of Staten Island also provides students with a tennis court, handball court, basketball court, and other various facilities that allow students to enjoy social activities outside of the classroom. For most people, including myself, these make the school much more enjoyable. There are some negatives that I believe the college has.

For one, there is a very limited amount of school spirit. Aside from the fraternities and sororities, sporting events don't receive much attention from the general student body. For most other schools, there is a lot more school unity that I believe the College Of Staten Island is lacking. Dormitories or the lack thereof, are also a problem. Although they are under construction, there won't be that many when it's completed. This, and the crowded parking spaces pose a problem for the many students who commute to the school.

The CUNY system, specifically the College Of Staten Island is overall very good for students. The negative aspects can all be fixed, while still providing the special qualities that make the school home to thousands of students every semester.

M.B.

MATT'S CLASSMATES RESPOND

What I'm hearing throughout Matthew's life essay is people, especially teachers, reminding him that he is not living up to his potential. This is the theme of the essay. I've heard this numerous times in my life also, as well as little witticisms, such as "He's a late bloomer." Matthew states: "the most common thing I heard from teachers in High School was my potential to be very smart, but that it was up to me to put in the effort." What bothers me the most was his lack of effort being directly related to his friendship with undesirable characters, the kinds of people with criminal intent, and whose behavior would destine them for prison, with a potential to drag down their friends along with them.

This had the deleterious ramification of emotionally upsetting his mother, and causing additional strain on her life. His mother, having experience the ravages of poverty, did not want the same turbulence visited upon her son. "Even though it would break my heart to see my mom get upset, I found it extremely difficult to break my habits." But this movie about the first segment of Matthew's life is heading towards a happy ending. Matthew's studies at the College of Staten Island are going very well now as he heads toward graduation, and his mother is so proud of him.

"The CUNY system, despite its flaws, was very effective for me. I don't have many of the issues that most other students do. Once you enter college, it's more of what you make of it then what is provided for you." In this statement Matt could have summed up his educational experiences both positive and his choices not so positive. Matt, let your mother read this.

I agree with Terence and the quote he choose. I also agree with Matt and that at the end of the day school and one's entire education is entirely on what YOU decide to make of it regardless on which institution you go to.

Matthew has come a long way and I find his story inspirational.

I agree with Terrance, it is all about what you put into it. We may have complaints about the system but there are always useful things we can take out of the experience. Mother's Day is coming up, wrap this and give it to her!

The story of your education has had its ups and downs, from winning the spelling contest to not being able to get into the school you had your hopes on for college. You mention in high school that "cheating on exams was widespread, and people often relied on this over studying." This was also an issue in my high school when I was younger, and I really have a bone to pick with this! How is it that we try so hard, and yet the valedictorian in high school is typically the person we all know was cheating (well, at least, this was the case in the school I attended). The worst part is, is that these students who make it by through cheating on tests often get into these grand universities. The typical platitude applies to this case, though: "Life is not fair!"

I enjoyed how you delved into your family's past to write your piece – it was interesting to read about your mother's past and her decisions to make it to where she is. While she faced quite a journey, it is clear that you are currently facing a journey of your own.

The great motivation in Mathew's educational experience is his mother. His mother encountered many hardships in her life. Mathew recognizes these hardships and believes his mother's sacrifices have paved the way for him to achieve. When reading his story it touches on the family bonds that help all of us develop in life. Whether it is your mother, father, brother, sister, aunt or uncle you can learn a lot from the life experiences of family members.

I can relate to you Matt because the support of a family can help a person go a long way in life. From your experiences I can tell you appreciate that very much.

"Matthew was eventually able to get back on track with a newfound passion for school, and years of regret for not finding it sooner." Don't regret it because you found it!

CHAPTER 4:

MEGHAN CONANAN

"All I really need to know about how to live, and what to do, and how to be, I learned in kindergarten. Wisdom was not at the top of the graduate school mountain, but there in the sand pile at school." Even the highest of educated men and women can connect to this poem by Robert Fulgham. Meghan is no different, she didn't graduate from an Ivy League school, but her life experiences along with schooling, have led her to the conclusion that life is truly based on core fundamental concepts; the same concepts that Robert Fulgham writes about in his poem.

What is the purpose of being educated if we don't know how to live with those around us? Sure you could end up being the wealthiest woman in the world, but without social skills whom will you have to enjoy your good fortunes with? "Share everything, play fair, don't hit people, and say sorry when you hurt somebody." The Golden Rule is taught thoroughly to our children, however Meghan learned that this simple rule somehow gets lost as children grow to adults. Leaders of governments and major corporations may have prevented some of the most notorious collapses, had they remembered: "don't take things that aren't yours, put things back where you found them, and clean up your own mess." Even the most common concepts of personal hygiene and a balanced life are taught. What happens to all of this, as we grow older?

After all of the competition one faces her whole life from school, to sports, to jobs, it's easy to forget one of the most fundamental rules that is spoken about in the poem. "When you go out in the world, watch out for traffic, hold hands and stick together." After all of the assignments written, lectures given, and tests taken it comes down to one thing. No matter what your age is, or what

university you attended, when you go out into the world, you will benefit the most in life when you realize that you still have to hold hands and stick together in order to survive. Various educational programs around the world can brag about enriching your learning and taking you above all of the rest, however in life we're all the same and need each other to survive. We need to learn to accept that fact, and also that fact that people learn things in different ways. If we continued to practice all of the rules that we were taught as children, the world would be a better place. A bachelors, masters, and doctorate are very prestigious achievements, but when it comes down to basics, everything we truly need to know we already learned in kindergarten.
M.C.

ALL I REALLY NEED TO KNOW I LEARNED IN KINDERGARTEN

Working with children can be extremely fulfilling, which is why I took a position at an after school center four years ago. My 5th grade class allows me to reflect upon how I dealt with social and educational issues when I was their age. As I watch them struggle and overcome their hardships, it's like a flashback. The girls will argue and not speak for the rest of the month; the boys will fight and then be best friends the minute after. They hate going home, needing a parent's signature on a failed spelling test, and they will begin to stress about the City and State tests starting in the beginning of September. They allow me to see things from a different perspective, and it's frightening, because in them I can see myself.

Reflecting on my past schooling, helped reveal how I came to be the person I am today. However, my time in school was not the sole factor in molding me into the person I am. My life experiences were extremely influential, and the hands on learning that came from them added to my development.

As a young child I often struggled in school. I was intelligent but my problem was that I was lazy. I can recall crying at homework time, and whining about how I didn't want to go to school because it was too much work. For all of the negative things that I remember I can also recall my most fun experiences. I loved doing projects during school, I can remember learning about Native Americans and building long houses out of glue and Popsicle sticks. I loved being creative and the fact that I can still recall doing those activities must mean that the assignments had an impact on me. Most of my younger years are all similar. I hated doing any schoolwork at home, I was only excited by creative projects, and I struggled with the idea of responsibility.

My 5th grade teacher helped snap me into shape. For my first four years of school I was placed in regular level classes. Towards the end of the 4th grade I was pulled into the hallway and told I would be put into the "advanced" 5th grade class. I wish I knew then, how much of an impact those words would have on the rest of my life.

As a ten year old, being pulled into a class, where most of the other kids had been together since kindergarten, was intimidating. Luckily I was accepted by the others and fit in socially, but my maturity was not on the same level. I suppose my teacher recognized this and realized I needed to be challenged. To this day I credit her for my work ethic.

I became so focused and matured so much at that age. She was known for being a fabulous teacher because she was very "by the book and old school," and she helped her students establish responsibility. That year I entered her class with not nearly as much maturity and responsibility as I left with. She prepared me to go into the scary world that was known as junior high school in the New York City public school system.

Thanks to her influence on my maturity, junior high was my favorite years of schooling. I loved the freedom that junior high gave me. Having different classes like cooking, art, and music was very refreshing and made me enjoy learning. I was able to balance my responsibility of schooling along with the challenges of a growing adolescent. I was growing up, but had I never been placed in that advanced class, I might have struggled with the freedom. I'm not sure that I would have been able to step up to the challenge to take responsibility for what I was doing, both academically and socially.

I consider my maturity from 5th grade through 8th to be the foundation of my educational career, and probably the most important. The way I went about studying for tests, doing homework, and writing papers throughout high school and college, was determined by the lessons I learned while maturing in grammar school.

I had an interesting high school career. I went to a high school that wasn't very popular; and I was separated from my childhood friends. What I found interesting about this specific time in my education was that I was making a transfer from public school to Catholic school. I was expecting to be challenged in a private school, but was sadly mistaken. I had one of the highest averages in my grade by the end of freshman year. Many of the things that were challenging to my classmates were actually just a repeat of things I had already learned in public school. I found this interesting because public school wasn't held in such high esteem. This opened my eyes and made me value my public school education. My classmates were proud of the names of their Catholic grammar schools, I was proud of my public school education.

I came to another realization while reflecting on my past, by looking at my later high school years. I realize that the three years after my freshman year, I settled into my environment. I was still responsible and did my work, however I found my laziness had returned. It was easy to just settle for a passing grade, because the standards weren't set high for me.

In public school I was placed in an advanced class for four years and worked extremely hard for my education. Once I entered Catholic school I was no longer given the challenge. I blended in with everyone and since they were happy with a mediocre education, I was too. At times I wonder, had I not chosen the Catholic school and continued in a public school, would I have been shaped even more differently? Had I been continuously challenged, would I have ended up attending a different college and pursuing a different career?

I don't harbor any ill feelings towards my Catholic high school. I managed to win the scholar athlete award during my senior year for maintaining the highest average for a student athlete my last year. I also gained more respect and learned more about my religion. Catholic school reinstated my love for structure and order, I find I perform better when everything is controlled and in order.

Senior year of high school I was forced to think about my future. My mother graduated from CSI and became a nurse, so schooling was always something that she pushed on me. She always stressed the importance of good grades.

My father dropped out of John Jay College and enlisted in the navy and is now a Chief in the New York City Sanitation Department. I consider my father to be one of the smartest people I know. He was always the one who would help me with homework and studying. He is extremely knowledgeable in a variety of fields. He would always tell me how he was extremely lucky. He managed to rise up the ranks to a high paying position without a college degree. However, he always wished he stayed at college. He always wonders what he could have become with a college degree. He claims that wasted knowledge is the saddest thing. He knows that he had the potential to become so much more. That's the reason why he suggested my sisters and I go to college after high school.

In September I began attending the College of Staten Island with the hopes of becoming a history teacher. I enjoy the structure of college classes that are taken by freshman and sophomores. The old fashioned lecture and teach method is one that I always seem to do best with. I appreciated taking COR and almost all of my 200 and 300 level history courses, since they were requirements for my major. I also appreciated taking Spanish for three semesters. Many students complained about the requirement of taking a foreign language, but I feel that it helped my education. I found learning about the structures of a different language helped me learn about the structure of English. This was sadly not given high importance in any of my other schools.

I was not in favor of the classes that used group work and discussions as their backbone. Most of my education classes were structured this way and I often found myself dreading having to go to class. In one education class a group of us (six or seven people), had to sit in the center of the classroom while the rest of the class listened. It was a method called "fish bowling." The students who were not responsible for discussing the topic at hand had to listen and critique the students that were talking about it. During one of these sessions a girl hadn't opened her mouth once to participate with the group, and was later on picked apart by the class as to what she was doing wrong.

I hated how they made her feel and when it came around to my turn in the fish bowl, all I could think of was "please God don't let me freeze up." I don't perform well in front of an audience, and I found it to be extremely intimidating. I ended up participating in the discussion, but not nearly as much as the others, and of course I was critiqued. The professor in charge of the class had taught for many years, and he obviously knew what he was doing. However, I'll never look back on that experience and recall what I learned in the class. Instead, I'll just remember being worried and nervous.

This opened my mind to realize that not everybody learns the same way. I'm sure some of the people in that class will remember the lessons learned while in that "fish bowl" but others will just remember the nerves. Not everybody is vocal, and just because someone is quiet in a class doesn't mean that he/she isn't learning. I understand that professors want their students to participate, and I would have been fine had it been in a "lecture" setting. I just didn't find the experience to be positive and I felt the negative feelings that I was having ruined the whole learning environment. Maybe I enjoy the "chalk and talk" method more than others because it gets directly to the point. I like having hard facts and being able to reflect about them, on my own. I can work in groups, but feel I learn more when I figure things out for myself. My shyness also probably plays a part in why I don't enjoy "community work." I stress over having to open up to others, instead of concentrating on learning.

A college class that I found very rewarding was my 300 level Imperialism course. My professor was excellent and she structured her class in a very orderly fashion. We would have a quiz in the beginning of class, and then a discussion about the readings either in groups or with her. That would be followed by her lecture and note taking and I appreciated that she knew what she was teaching. The class would finish with a movie or audio clip, something pertaining to the particular lesson for the day. For me this was a perfectly balanced structure. Starting with a quiz on what we had learned previously, to refresh our minds, then participation, and then note taking, and ending with some technological assistance. The movie or audio at the end was the perfect way to create an imprint in our brains about what we had learned during the lesson.

At the beginning of my junior year of college, I made the best decision of my life. I decided that I would study abroad in Australia for six months. It was a challenge to afford it, but my hard work and determination helped earn the money. When I made the decision not to travel away to college, I decided I would at some point spend a semester abroad. Going to Australia was the best decision I had ever made, and taught me so many things about life as well as myself. It taught me lessons that can't be taught from books or in class rooms. This hands on life experience was the best type of education I was ever taught.

I decided to travel to Australia alone. No one else from Staten Island accompanied on my trip, and I knew no one once I got there. It was literally a whole new world, one where I had to learn to meet new people and adapt to their culture. Living on my own was the hardest part because I had lived at home for 20 years. I didn't find it difficult to take care of myself; I just found it very lonesome, coming from a house filled with people. Luckily I met some great friends from all over the world who were in the same situation. Getting away from home and seeing how different, not only the world was, but other people were, was eye opening for me.

While at the University of Newcastle I took a course on the history of Australian Aboriginals. This was one of the most enlightening classes I have ever taken in my life. Little is known in America about these people, and my ignorance amazed me. As I sat in a class taught by an Aboriginal man I was shocked to hear that the treatment the Aboriginal people had received were the same as African Americans. I continuously couldn't understand why Aboriginals were being referred to as "blacks"; because they weren't as dark as the "blacks" that I had seen all my life. This class opened my eyes to the undeniable fact that race is a man-made thing, and that color had nothing to do with it. This particular group of people was being treated in the same exact way African Americans had been, and the reason was the same man-made excuse... because they were "black." When I think about the lessons I learned in Australia and the ones I learned at home, being an historian isn't everything I thought it would be. I used to think being an historian meant just learning about facts and events and remembering them, being able to pass them on so that people never forgot what happened in the past.

I now realize that being an historian is about being able to connect the events that happen in the past to different groups of people, in the past and present in order to better understand why we do the things we do. Being able to draw connections in my head between two separate groups of people, without learning it from a textbook was proof that I had been educated. No one sat in that Australian classroom with me saying, "Oh look this is similar to the history of African Americans in your country." I was able to link the two historical stories together, given the facts of both groups, and that to me was the best form of education. Through that I was able to see that regardless of how far away we live from each other, and how different we think we are, the human brain somehow works in the same ways.

Of course petting kangaroos and snorkeling in Australia's beautiful waters were highlights, but my time in their University system was just as fulfilling. They structure things differently than we do in the United States. Each course you take is split into 2 different sections. First is a lecture, which you have the option to attend, followed by a tutorial, which is mandatory. The lectures are given in big lecture halls, generally with a different tutor giving a lesson each week. After the lecture you proceed to a classroom where you meet with a tutor to discuss the lecture and review for tests and assignments. Another thing I found interesting was the informality expected at the university. I never once referred to my tutor as Professor Downs, instead he was always referred to as Matt.

I also found how they value schooling interesting. I had met friends outside of the University and was completely shocked to find out that the majority of Australians don't actually go to college after high school. In America, you are frowned upon and put into a different social class if you don't have a degree. In Australia, they couldn't grasp what I was trying to explain, because the majority of people go to high school and then find a job; it's the minority that is strange and decides to continue on to college. Seeing how happily they lived made me question everything I was taught. In America we're taught you live to work and get the best paying job, therefore you need a lot of schooling. In Australia it is important to work, but your life doesn't revolve around it. They don't worry about if their neighbor has a bigger house and nicer car. Their relaxed and carefree way of life made me question what I was doing spending all of my time and money in a classroom.

In reality does all of my schooling and education make me a better person? If it does then what does that say about them? They were some of the happiest people I have ever met and surely just living life was educational enough for them. I see myself now as a very structured and orderly person who has a very creative side, and I like to think that my education and schooling helped frame that. However, when I think of the Australians that I met who didn't have the same education as myself, they were just as intelligent and happy, so I started to question if education came from the books and lessons, or if it came from something else.

The fact that I can question things that are supposed to be just accepted leads me to believe that I have developed into the person I wanted to become. All throughout college they teach you that you will no longer be fed information and simply expected to retain it. In college you are given information and are expected to question it, which is what I feel I'm doing. After I graduate I don't expect to stop learning. The life experiences that I will continue to have will also make me question the norm, and add to my desire for learning, furthering my life long education.

And as for CUNY and CSI (Attempting to Learn, Forgetting to Live)

Reflecting on your educated career makes you wonder, was it all necessary? If the answer is yes, then what is the reason? You are a product of your society, regardless of how much an individual can claim to be unique and special, society will dictate your life.

The most substantial evidence for this theory can be found in traveling. My travels have allowed me to see that different cultures and societies don't hold education to the same standards. My time spent in Australia was an eye opener. Australians live life completely differently from Americans. In America you are looked down upon if you do not pursue a higher education. In Australia it is the social norm to graduate college and go straight to a full time job. There isn't the same pressure on 18 year olds once their mandatory schooling ends. I was also fortunate to form friendships with people from England, and France. My English friend stated that the majority of her friends did not attend university and it was perfectly normal; this shocked me. My French friend was shocked at how young I was because many Europeans take time to travel after high school, for a couple of years, and then attend university. In America none of this is acceptable. These cultures have stated that it is ok to simply have a high school education and continue to do whatever you desire, the complete opposite of what Americans are taught.

American children are taught from a young age that they should go to primary school, then continue on to high school, and lastly university because this is the way that they will obtain a good job, earn money, and live a happy life. I have seen how happy and stress free Australians live, their lives are not perfect yet they are not in constant competition with each other. Australians live life exactly how they want to, there is no brainwashing at a young age to convince them that a higher education will bring them happiness. My education has taught me to question the norms, and seeing how content the Australian people are opened my eyes to realize that being educated only makes you happy because society has stated it should.

My problems are with society and not the CUNY system and CSI itself. Society stated that I would be a failure without a degree, therefore I was able to afford the tuition for my education, and able to obtain that degree. I was grateful to have a close and cheap program near home. I was a product of society, I fell right into the pattern that everyone does, and didn't want to be looked down upon as an uneducated nobody. If society was unbiased and didn't have opinions on educated vs. uneducated, I'm not too sure that I would have continued onto the college level. It seems that as the years go on society becomes more demanding of education. In my grandparents era they needed a high school diploma to find work, for my parents it was a college degree, and now almost any job requires a masters at some point. Pretty soon we will be spending all of our lives in school, attempting to learn and forgetting to live.
M.C.

MEGHAN'S CLASSMATES RESPOND

Well Meghan, as they say in Australia, "GA DA, Matc." I've known for a long time the kind of treatment that has been meted out to their Aboriginal people. I disagree however, with their comparison to our country's African American population. To me, their Aboriginal populace is more analogous to our American Indian people. The primary reason being is American Indians are the only people who are classified in America as a "native" people. Similarly, Aboriginals are the only people "native" to Australia. They are both indigenous peoples.

Certainly your experience of learning about a different lifestyle in Australia would ring true with Henry Adams as knowledge acquired by experiencing life's journey. Australians have always had a reputation for being and easy-going, fun-loving, people who love drinking beer. Fosters brand puts American beer to shame. And, what would you expect from a group of people with so much Gaelic ancestry, being Scotch, Irish and Welsh. Seriously, it's obvious they enjoy life more than Americans do.

I feel your father's angst and disappointment concerning not finishing college. I was forced to drop out of college in 1975. I've had a desire to finish my degree for over thirty years. Like your father, I worked for the City of New York with some measure of success. You seem to have a well-balanced life on the horizon for you.

It's good to finally read about an educational success story in Meghan, starting in the fifth grade and laying the foundation for junior high and a positive experience. The continued criticisms of Catholic schools shows that the badly needed resources available to public schools should be made available to Catholic schools. I can't help to think how much better the Catholic schools might be if the tax dollars available to public schools were also made available to Catholic schools. Megan has taken full advantage of CUNY in her trip to Australia, where she gained insight to another culture.

I really hope there comes a time when all colleges require students to go for a semester abroad. Just as your insights changed because you were brought into a new country with attitudes different than what you're accustomed to in the States, this has shaped you into a more mature person. Being from different nations myself, I can't help but notice many people don't realize there is another world out there other than the American way which makes them self-centered and ignorant.

It's refreshing to hear about teachers who truly care about their students such as your 5th grade teacher did. Too often teachers forget about that aspect of schooling, and instead they expect their students all to be similar in their learning. Sometimes students need that extra push from an authority figure besides their parents; unfortunately it just isn't always there.

Meghan! This was a very enjoyable read for me. I, too, enjoyed my time in junior high school with great classes such as art, cooking, and sewing--home economics classes! It was truly saddening when the public schools started taking these classes away from the students. Because of these classes, I learned how to cook and sew! But at the same time, it is arguable that these classes are simply things of the past that needed to be discarded to make way for a more "valuable" education for students.

I can understand why you found the "fish bowl" method of conversing as "putting you on the spot." I can agree with that. Still, it is a method used in classrooms nowadays. Whether it's really so effective or not is questionable, and I can certainly agree that it can feel ostracizing, especially when you are being, or feel as if you are being, judged for your own personal opinions.

Your experience abroad and your response to your time in Australia were quite interesting. You mention the idea of Aboriginal "blacks" vs. African American "blacks" [in America]; that "[t]his class opened my eyes to the undeniable fact that race is a man-made thing, and that color had nothing to do with it." It was truly interesting to me when you realized your Americacentric way of thinking, and saw the way of life that is different in other societies. It seems the experience abroad really was a great experience that truly affected your education.

Meghan has totally transformed herself through her years in school. She was lazy in her past but in the present she is active in her education. She states "The fact that I can question things that are supposed to be just accepted leads me to believe that I have developed into the person I wanted to become." This statement reveals that Meghan has developed intellectually. Questions are of great value and if you do not question anything, you will fall for everything. Meghan has come a long way in her education. This statement is proof of her positive transformation.

Wow. What a great story! I can identify with you on everything you wrote -minus the travelling abroad. But questioning is something that I also have come to do in my adult years, and to me that is also my definition of reaching what I wanted. So really, what does this mean for our educational system and the expectations of society? Would I not have become an adult who learned to question and critically analyze life if it had not been for college? I think not. Like you I wish to live life like the Australian people, not worrying about making the most money with the best job to have the biggest and best things. This is a mantra I have adopted literally within the last few months, so I thank you for writing this and reaffirming what I have been trying to do with my life! Meghan, I really loved your discussion of your early years in school. I always whined and cried and hated homework too (I still do). I also remember making long houses - it was one of my favorite projects.

Your semester in Australian must have been amazing! I have always wanted to go there.

I really admire your ability to step out of yourself and view the world from different points of view; I think it is a skill that will serve you well as a historian and in life.

CHAPTER 5:

MATT COOMBS

I was shocked after reading my own writing in this book. I have always had a negative viewpoint of school and would sum it up as "a waste of my time." I have an endless list of complaints that didn't even come up in this chapter and part of me wishes I would have ripped into the education system and my experience in it, as I often do verbally. However, I have recognized how this college has helped me and I don't want to sound like some of the people I would hear around campus, unfairly bashing the education system, specifically the College of Staten Island.

My mother always told me that my "education is what you make of it"; if you go in with a bad attitude, then you've already defeated yourself before you have even started. When I was writing about my education, I chose to write about the positive aspects of my education in the New York City Board of Education. Like most big organizations, they are not perfect. There is always some part of the system that lags behind the rest of the organization, but for the most part my experience in the education system was OK.
M.C.

TTAM

School was never Matt's "thing." For the most part he hated school. There was a glimmer of hope here and there where he took some interest in it, but it is safe to say he hated school.

Matt started school in 1990. It was same school his father and two older brothers also had attended. Matt would describe his experience there as the closest thing to a private education at the public's expense. The school, P.S. 26, had approximately thirty students to a class, one class to a grade, and went from kindergarten to fifth grade, two hundred students total in the whole school. The principal knew most of the students' names as well as their parents'. It was here that little Matthew J. Coombs started his uphill battle with education.

Kindergarten for the most part was a blur, literally. Matt couldn't see a thing. He was both near and far sided, but no one realized this just yet. Here is where he mastered his ABC's and 1 2 3's, but backwards. Turns out he was dyslexic. He then went into the first grade where the teacher sat him in the back of the class because he was one of the taller students. One day the class was tasked with copying a paragraph off of the chalkboard. It was this that led to the discovery of his vision problems. When the teacher checked Matt's work, she saw just a bunch of squiggly lines on the paper. At first thought she thought he was messing around, but later realized he couldn't see a thing and just wrote what he saw. His fight with education just got harder.

Matt was in the third grade before he had learned something substantial, but he didn't learn it in school. One night while watching the nightly news on he saw a news clip of a man being dragged by his tied hands through the streets being kicked and stepped on. Matt knew what he was watching wasn't right; that people shouldn't be doing this to that man on the TV. It made him uncomfortable but he didn't really understand what he was seeing. He knew it was evil and wicked. It turns out that what Matthew saw was the body of United States Staff Sgt. William David Cleveland being dragged through the streets of Mogadishu, Somalia during the Battle of Mogadishu in 1993. Here was where Matthew learned what evil was and how horrific men could be to one another.

During Matt's years in P.S. 26 he was placed into Resource Room because of his dyslexia. Once a day, for an hour or so, Matt and a few other students with similar problems would leave the main class of thirty and go to Resource Room. Here is where the New York City Board of Education drilled and reinforced primary reading, writing, and math skills to help the struggling Matt overcome his dyslexia. Years later, Matt would look back at this time and feel as though his education here was comparable to a private school education. There was so much group and individual work between the few other Resource Room students and the teacher that it provided the students with the extra help they needed to keep them at the same pace as the rest of the class. It turns out that Matt's school's small size was beneficial. Most other schools in Staten Island did not have this level of individual help for students with learning disabilities. He was very fortunate to have this education and extra help but it was only when he became a man that he was able to appreciate it.

In the fourth grade, history started to stand out at as one of the more interesting subjects to Matt. Here he was tasked with a Social Studies Fair project. With help from his mother, he erected an American Indian long house, which was common to local Indians that used to inhabit Staten Island. Matt also started the music program in fourth grade. He wanted to play the drums but was assigned the trombone. Matt had a good ear for music, but because of his dyslexia, he had a very hard time reading musical notation. To Matt, it was like learning to read a different language. He had enough problems with his first language! He got by in music class just by listening to what the other boy who played the trombone would play and he would replicate the music while pretending to read the musical notes. He had a keen ability to hear music played and be able to replicate it. This would later help him in high school when he pursued learning the guitar.

Fourth grade was also where Matthew received the best punishment ever, "The Charts!" His teacher Mr. Gray would assign "The Charts" to a student when he or she would get in trouble. What the student would have to do was write out the multiplication chart, or the times tables, anywhere between five and ten times. This turned out to be one of the best things for the young Matt. To this day, he still thanks Mr. Gray for giving him "The Charts" because it helped him in his struggle with school.

Fifth grade was a pivotal year in school for Matt. It was here where he figured out that one could not do his school work and still get pushed to the next grade. All year long Matt sat in the back row of the class with two other students. They had seven or eight desks to split amongst them and store all their, for a lack of a better word, crap, in them. They had all their papers just jammed packed in their desk, and in Matt's case it was filled with failed spelling tests and incomplete homework that he never did or never turned in. He never studied for a spelling test or anything else for that matter. He would always just scrape by. His parents tried their best to motivate him and get him to do his school work, but still young Matt would do just enough work to get by.

On one particular failed spelling test of Matthew's, Mr. Frank, his fifth grade teach held up a piece of paper while sitting at his desk in the front of the room and called out "MR. COOMBS!" Matt looked up and said, "Yes?" "Do you know what I have in my hands Mr. Coombs?" Matt could see that he was holding a spelling test with a big fat zero on it in red. He looked at Mr. Frank and said, "A spelling test with a zero on it?" "Wrong," Mr. Frank said, "It's YOUR spelling test with a zero on it." Mr. Frank then waved the zero around and said, "We're not going to hold you back, but you're not going to like the class you're placed in at junior high." If you were to see Matt and ask him about what Mr. Frank said, Matt would tell you Mr. Frank was right, he didn't like where he was placed. Mr. Frank had taught Matt a very valuable lesson, don't slack off.

In the sixth grade, Matthew was placed in a low-level class. It wasn't special education or anything, but he was the only white student in the class. He was not used to being the odd man out. This class had the reputation of being the most poorly-behaved class and Matt hated it. This was a complete wake up call to the young Matthew. He worked as hard as he could in school to do better than all the other students but it was of no use. Although he was the best and smartest student in the class, his hard work didn't pay off. Once you were in the bad class, you stayed in the bad class. When 7th grade rolled around he was still in the same class with the troublesome students who would pick on him, but this year he learned to stand up for himself.

The other students tried to pick on Matt and make fun of him, but little did they know that Matt had two older brothers, seven and nine years older than him. Matt would routinely try to fight them like most little brothers try to do and failed, resulting in his being able to take a beating pretty well. Matt wasn't scared to fight but preferred not to, and he wasn't easily provoked. Matt was never upset or hurt by what bullies would say, but if you physically hurt him, it was a completely different story. One bully tried to fight Matt one day and provoked him by snapping a rubber band on Matt's neck while he was doing his class work in math class. Like a bull in a china shop, Matt proceeded bounce the wrongdoer off every desk and punch him and bloody his nose in front of the entire class. Matt never got in trouble for this because the teacher had witnessed the whole thing. She saw this student provoke Matt and she had felt that he deserved it. This of course wouldn't happen in today's classrooms. But this fight had worked out in his favor. The rest of the class learned that you should watch out for the quiet ones. Matt never had any problems with bullies from this point on in his education. By eighth grade, Matt had fully developed a hatred for school. The only thing he enjoyed about it was the few friends he had made and the chorus he sang in, though it gave him a terrible case of stage fright that sticks with him till this day.

Matt's interest in history started outside of school, but there wasn't one specific thing or event that sparked it. If you were to ask him what piqued his interest he would say his parents and the countless trips to historical sites around the country the family would take. He loved them! His most memorable trip with his parents was in the eighth grade to see a reenactment of the Battle of Gettysburg in Gettysburg, Pennsylvania. Here was where Matt's interest in United States political, military, and technological history began.

By the time he entered Port Richmond High School, Matt would consume anything with historical value that would satisfy his inquisitive interest about the past. He took a particular interest in anything related to World War II, especially after seeing the movie *Saving Private Ryan*. Momentum was added to his growing passion with the release of HBO's miniseries *Band of Brothers*. He wished he could be these heroes portrayed in the films. To satisfy his fantasy, he started to collect military medals, pins, buttons, period equipment, tools, knives, uniforms, documents, anything he would get his hands on. Matt felt that when he held an old medal, a sailor's dog tags, or a Marine's knife, it connected him to a time in American history when Americans were viewed as heroes by the people of the world, not imperialistic villains raping countries of their wealth or toppling foreign governments as he was later taught in college by his leftist teachers. He longed to be part of what he viewed as a golden age in America, a pivotal time in American history that he could capture through his collecting of these items.

High school is also where he learned to appreciate the fine art of classical music, particularly classical guitar. With the help of a teacher and some other interested students, they started a guitar ensemble. This was one of two main attractions of school for the teenage Matt. The other was the office where he worked during his lunch period. Here was where he started to learn what he would later depend upon for a living, his IT computer work. He would help set up the computers in the high school offices and classrooms, as well as configure computers for users. He didn't think much more of it at time than a personal hobby. Matt, the teenager would have never guessed that fixing and repairing computers would be his main skill in life from this point in time. He thought he was going to go to college and become the next Indiana Jones.

Matt stuck with Resource Room until he graduated from high school. By this time the special education administrators recommended that he no longer be in the program. He hadn't showed signs of dyslexia since P.S. 26, but was just on the lower end of the good student spectrum. Matt was lazy and would rather do anything else other than school work. The real reason Matt stuck with Resource Room was because it gave him an easy way out of getting a Regent's Diploma. If you were in Resource Room you were not required to get a Regent's Diploma. Instead you could receive a standard high school diploma. Matt knew he wouldn't be able to pass his math Regent's test, and he was right. He passed every test they gave him, all the histories, all the sciences, all the English and reading tests, but the math test he failed. And his SAT score was embarrassing. He didn't think anything of it. He didn't really care.

The College of Staten Island was an eye opening experience for the better. No one cared if Matt came to class or not. If he didn't have his homework done, no one called his house or sent letters home. It may be because he was older or maybe this was really what he needed, but once everyone was off his back, he started to take school seriously. Matt was able to see the error of his ways and realized he did himself a disservice by not taking school seriously. Although he was enjoying going to school he saw that he really wasn't prepared to do college level reading and writing.

While in a remedial writing class Matt's teacher asked a student to read his work aloud. After the student read his rather embarrassing poorly written work, the teacher politely said his work didn't make sense, to which the student replied, "I dink it do." It was at that moment Matt became horrified and embarrassed to be sitting in a remedial class. He was even more embarrassed when he realized he didn't know the difference between there, their, and they're, or would say things like "me and Mike go to the store" when it should be "Mike and I went to the store." This opened his eyes to how stupid he had made himself, and he set out to correct it. Matt worked hard to improve his writing skills and because he decided to become a history major, all the reports he went on to write honed his writing skills.

One of the first big assignments the young man needed to complete was assigned by Professor Calvin Holder. Even though Matt disagreed politically with him, Matt very much liked Professor Holder. Professor Holder didn't put you down or make you feel dim-witted. Matt tended to shy away from people whom he disagreed with politically. Politics had always been a hot button subject for him and he tended to get worked up and loud. On the first day of Professor Holder's class, he told the students they had a ten-page report due at the end of the semester on anything in United States history from 1865 to the present. It was like a dream come true for

Matt. He could finally do school work on a subject that greatly interested him, World War II. Matt was nervous and scared. He had never written a paper of that length before. He decided that he was going to focus on the Battle of the Bulge that took place in the Ardennes Forest in Belgium. He wrote a paragraph or two for three to four weeks and by the end of the term, when everyone else was panicking to get their report finished, Matt's paper was all done and ready to be handed in. He passed the class with a B average and tended to continue the trend of getting Bs throughout his college career. Looking back, Matt realized that the paper he was so proud of wasn't as good as he remembered. His writing and researching skills have come a long way since Professor Holder's class, but it was the first substantial paper he had written and he is still proud of it today.

By this time, Matt's hobby with computers really took hold of him. He started to build high end computers to run top of the line video games, as well as pirating anything and everything he could find on the internet. Matt often described the internet, before government involvement and regulation, as the closest thing to the "Wild West" he could experience. The internet had it all and he loved it. He loved it so much that he switched from the College of Staten Island to DeVry University because he felt CSI's Software Programming courses were old and outdated. It took $45,000 and two years for Matt to discover that he is a kinesthetic learner[1], and not a mathematical thinker. He dropped out of DeVry and was hired by and

---

[1] Kinesthetic learning is a learning style in which learning takes place by the student actually carrying out a physical activity, rather than listening to a lecture or merely watching a demonstration. People with a kinesthetic learning style are also commonly known as do-ers. According to proponents of the learning styles theory, students who have a predominantly kinesthetic learning style are thought to be natural discovery learners: they have realizations through doing, as opposed to having thought first before initiating action. They may struggle to learn by reading or listening (links to dyslexia). When learning it helps for the student to move around as this increases the students' understanding with learners generally getting better marks in exams when they use that style. The kinesthetic learner usually does well in things such as chemistry experiments, sporting activities, art and acting. They also may listen to music while learning or studying. It is common for kinesthetic learners to focus on two different things at the same time. They will remember things by going back in their minds to what their body was doing. They also have very high hand-eye coordination and very quick receptors.

later managed a computer shop for the next three years which had always been his dream. He always said that he wanted to finish his bachelor's in history but he enjoyed working and making money more than school. He promised himself that one day, sooner or later, he would return to the College of Staten Island and finish up his degree.

Work was great! Matt loved managing the computer shop in Staten Island. Here is where he sharpened his sales and customer service skills and learned how to deal with people on a professional business level. He learned to manage the day to day operations of a small business and how to manage people under him. But the economy had different plans for the business where he worked. Money became tight and the owners parted ways. Shortly after this split, Matt left the shop, enrolled at the College of Staten Island, and started working there part time in the IT department. The promise that he made to himself of finishing his degree in history could now be fulfilled.

Matt often wondered what might have happened to him if his dyslexia wasn't discovered. When he was in high school, a friend gave him a book written about a local mobster whose old house Matt would pass daily. He only had interest in the book because it was about a local person. He disliked how people glorified the mafia, especially people living in Staten Island. The book was about Sammy "the Bull" Gravano's life growing up and his entry into crime. What he discovered reading the book was that Gravano was dyslexic as well. Because this was back in the 50s and 60s, the school system didn't know how to handle this problem. They basically labeled him retarded and were unable to help him. He then turned to hanging out with the wrong crowds in school which lead to his life in organized crime.

Matthew walked away from this book very thankful that his learning disability had been diagnosed. He could only wonder where his life could have taken him if his dyslexia went undiagnosed. By the time he had reached twenty-seven years old, Matt realized that his dyslexia, as his doctor thinks, was an undiagnosed case of Attention Deficit, and had always been holding him back from doing well in school. Yes, it is true that

Matt is no longer writing letters and words backwards, but his learning disability is what kept him from focusing on and completing his school work. It truly wasn't his fault, he wasn't lazy, uninterested, or stupid, but rather he just had a hard time doing schoolwork because of circumstances out of his control. It wasn't until he was older that Matt realized he didn't actually hate school.

And as for CSI and CUNY

My education stopped once I stopped writing letters backwards. After that, school just became a state-forced babysitting service. Yes, I learned about history and science, but I still am awful at math and I hate to read. I went to school every day because, by law, my attendance was required. I spent most of high school fist fighting friends in our own fight club and pursuing my own interests. All I have learned in life can be credited to my mother and father. Countless lessons on living a good life as a good person were provided to me by them. Both my parents taught me to be extremely handy, which plays into my learning disability and my kinesthetic learning style.

Another big part of education in life was provided to me by the Boy Scouts of America. In Boy Scouts I learned many things other than just tying knots. Many of the merit badges were designed to make each Boy Scout well rounded in many areas a life. To earn some of the badges, we were required to shoot guns. While earning others, we learned about budgeting money and fiscal responsibility. Scouting was very important to me and many other young men. It taught us skills for life.

To this day I still have trouble with spelling, to the point where I often become embarrassed. I recently had an experience where my father was sitting at the computer and asked me to spell a word for him. What word we were trying to spell I can't recall, but we were both scratching our heads trying to figure it out. We couldn't do it so we just picked a less fancy word and moved on. Right then and there I realized my father may have had some of the learning problems I have. I asked him about it and he agreed that he thought he might have had some of the same problems as me, but not to the degree I had them. The best way to describe my learning disability at the age of twenty-seven would be that I am an awful speller and have a low attention span, but as I told my dad that night we tried to spell together, "Who cares if I can spell or not, I have spell check."

I feel that many Staten Island residents do not realize or appreciate the educational gem that is the College of Staten Island. As I previously mentioned, students at the College of Staten Island always seem to talk bad about the college, but seem never really to have a legitimate reason as to why they dislike it. From what I can gather, it seems like most people here are lazy and don't want to work for their college degree. They have gotten used to people in the education system just pushing them through and not having to work to progress. My complaints about the system don't seem to fit in with the negative talk I hear around me. Read my experience in the New York City Board of Education and take from it the positive effects it had on just one of the students who went through the system.
M.C.

MATT'S CLASSMATES RESPOND

It was good to hear that Matt had experienced success in the diagnosing of his dyslexia, and was able to take advantage of the resources available to move forward in academia. I believe that Matt, in time will appreciate that the struggles he describes throughout his education will be the part that contributes the most to his education. Matt certainly seems to have effectively categorized the students who are most prone to complain about CSI as the ones looking to be hand-fed through college, I agree with Matt, it's time for them to "man-up" and get the education they want as well as need.

Matt had fought and won a battle with dyslexia. His hardships that he went through can only make him a stronger individually both in school and the real world. I also agree with him that many students expect CSI to basically give them free grades. School is an experience that you decide how you want the outcome to be.

"Ttam," by Mathew Coombs is an uplifting educational experience. Mathew and I were diagnosed with two different learning disabilities. I was diagnosed with Attention Deficit Disorder and internalized this disorder because it was given to me as a child. I began to lose my own identity not just through this label but through grades as well. I started to believe I'm not smart enough. This disorder was given by teachers and psychiatrists. Matt had dyslexia which means he would write and read words backwards. He benefited from the Resource Room to teach him how to overcome his learning disabilities. While my learning disability does not have a cure, I am truly happy that Matt benefitted from the educational system in helping him overcome his dyslexia. Though later I found out on my own I never had a learning disability, I had a learning ability which the educational system structure could not understand. I was never slow or not paying attention. I was learning at my own pace, in my own way. The educational systems process is narrow for individuals like myself and therefore I believe it fails. Resource room makes individuals lazy and gives excuses for students to do poorly. The Regents' exam is an example and Matt mentions it. All he had to do was just pass it with a 55 or 65 and he would not receive a Regent's diploma. I was in the same boat but my question is why are we getting extra attention and barely passing state exams? Why would they just pass us by, knowing that when we get to college it will be difficult? It is mentioned that Matt had to take remedial courses. If Matt would have been taught properly, never given the escape route of just passing a Regent's exam, he would have never taken remedial courses. Resource room isolates the students from their other peers allowing them to feel that somehow they are different. When the students find out why they are different and how they are different through a diagnoses that was given to them they begin to adapt to those differences. They internalize whatever is the behavior or stereotype of their diagnoses. This messes with the future and opportunities of the individual or student. Matt has a lot of positive energy in his paper, which is great. He has a wonderful personality and while reading his educational experience it shines through. Matt states "From what I can gather, it seems like most people here are lazy and don't want to work for their college degree. They have gotten used to people in the education system just pushing them through and not having to work to progress." I agree partially with Mathew's statement. I believe the blame would be the lower educational institutions. Matt states "They have gotten used to people in the educational system pushing them through." I would not blame the students; I would blame the system because they should have prepared them for college. These students are frustrated. I would not call them lazy but frustrated because they cannot break out of bad habits that were passed down to them through the lower educational institutions. They cannot grasp the material that's handed to them adequately and therefore the results in college are devastating for them. Since this occurs they complain because they are struggling and trying but feel they will not fulfill their own goal of receiving a college degree. Some drop out. Also college is not for everybody and some of those students that complain are forced by parents and society itself to go to college.

At the end of the story Matthew talks about Sammy "The Bull" Gravano's innocuous ignorance of his dyslexic condition. Due to the school authorities' own incomprehension, he was labeled retarded, and therefore a misfit. He therefore started hanging out with other social deviants, whose activities evolved into a life of crime. Mr. Gravano's tragedy of criminality could have been avoided if he had been properly diagnosed early in his school years.

Matthew, armed with this knowledge of his condition, was at least able to avoid being labeled as a menace to society, because he and the authorities knew he had a situation which required special assistance to enable him to assimilate into the country's social norms, instead of being persecuted with a label of "retarded."

When I worked for the City of New York for thirty-three years, upper-management would put up Human Resources slogans throughout its property espousing such things as, "Our employees are our most important resource." Although met with sarcastic derision from my fellow workers, that slogan is true. Mr. Gravano did not get the help he needed and he turned out for the worst. Mr. Coombs calls himself a political conservative. It is the Republican Party that destroys social welfare programs every chance they get, making it much more difficult for future childhood Matts to get the Human Resources care that they will need.

"From what I can gather, it seems like most people here are lazy and don't want to work for their college degree. They have gotten used to people in the education system just pushing them through and not having to work to progress." I can attest to this as I've discussed in my paper. I always did enough to get by, but I was rarely challenged to do more. It makes those students think less abstractly as they aren't being pushed to succeed, but rather just pushed through school.

"From what I can gather, it seems like most people here are lazy and don't want to work for their college degree. They have gotten used to people in the education system just pushing them through and not having to work to progress." I completely agree with this statement. Four years here and I feel that mostly that describes the type of fellow classmates I have been in contact with but not all of course. Matt you have overcome a lot with your struggles in school and I found your paper inspirational and very interesting.

I must begin by saying that I applaud you for beating up that bully and sticking up for yourself! It is interesting to read how you found yourself in the History major — your intense interest in the subject and enjoyment in visiting historical sights, as well as your distaste for reading and math. Your piece has taken the reader from your early stage as a child until the present. Lastly, I must add that the last sentence of your educational life story thus far was extremely witty. I was both amused and interested while I read about your experiences.

I agree with Matt's comment about "manning up." Too many students at CSI are only here because their mommies and daddies told them that they had to be. Therefore, they associate college with high school, just another thing they have to get through to make their parents happy. Once the students acquire a real hunger for learning at the university level, and attend classes because they desire to, I will be convinced that their intentions are genuine.

While Matt's educational journey is an interesting one, what intrigued me most is the realization that CSI was beneficial to him based on the fact that it had given him freedom within his own education. I feel this is a silver lining in the dark cloud that is CSI that deserves recognition. It is a proven approach actually. Here is a student that overcame dyslexia, taught himself two musical instruments, and yet all he really wanted was for the authorities to get off his back. I can relate to that notion. Catholic school teachers were constantly forcing me to do things, claiming it was "for my benefit," yet stepping into public school one of the first things I realized was that I was responsible for myself for the first time ever, and I excelled. This false pretense that people cannot take care of themselves actually makes people more lazy and reliant on others. Not to mention that the rewards of accomplishment when one has full independence is much more rewarding than completing a task because a superior told you it would benefit you. Therefore, I think Matt will agree with me when I say that receiving a college degree on my own gives me more pride and sense of accomplishment than anything else has to date in my 22 year life.

CHAPTER 6:

ZANA ISMAIL

From the beginning of her life Zana Ismail was always in a fight to continue her education. She felt like it was the right thing to do. In rereading her educational history it has become very clear to her that education is not intelligence, but that what an education can do is open your mind to a different level of knowledge. The reason Zana was able not to fall into the traditional ways of her family was because she believed she could do much more. No one in the family had the opportunity to complete high school and Zana wanted to set an example and show that gaining an education is more than just a degree. Looking back and considering the experiences she has encountered brought strength and prosperity to Zana, which helped to further her goals. To some people going to school or colleges seems like such a small issue. However, when you are told you can't or don't have too, pursue the education you want or even any education at all, you would then have a change of mind and fight for it. Zana's education was forever in doubt and she just wanted to finish to prove that she could and will accomplish what she sets out to do. What Zana did learn from her experiences is that education came to be a great privilege in life. Z.I.

THE LIFE & EDUCATION OF ZANA ISMAIL

I am at the end of my college education and I have learned a lot. I learned about the past and how to write about the past. However, I really do not know much of anything. Education and learning never end for the reason that we will always learn from new experiences. A person's education is not only what he learns formally in school but it is life experiences as well. Throughout a person's life he will encounter certain situations that will shape who he is, and each situation will be part of the forces that help that person determine his future.

My life isn't perfect and I am not a perfect person. However, I can say first that so far in my life I believe I have made the right decisions, not to sound self-absorbed or arrogant. I am a person who focuses on what I want and what I think is important for myself. I taught myself to be this kind of person because for all my life, certain family members discouraged my education, and so I thought I would not make as far as high school. Being an Arab American growing up in Brooklyn living with a big family was not easy. Still, it helped me to understand certain aspects of life that have proved to be important to me.

All through my adolescence, where I grew up and who my family was shaped my life. Growing up with my parents, my father's parents, his two brothers and my three siblings was difficult. Living with all these people and having other family members over every other day took a toll on all of us. This affected me for the reason that I was not getting the attention I needed as a child. My mother, who is a very sweet woman with beautiful brown eyes, was always so busy taking care of everyone in my household that she did not have the time to help me. I was falling behind in my schoolwork. During my first years of grade school I did not understand the material as fast as the other children and I always felt singled out, since I was the only one who seemed to be behind. My teachers were not as helpful as they should have been. Basic reading, writing and math seemed to be like climbing a mountain for me and even at that time I knew I had to help myself. Even though I was not the best in my class I always tried to be better and read more often as well as practice my math so I would not fall behind. I had an older cousin who would help me in certain subjects and with my schoolwork, since my mother was always busy with the family. Looking back now I understand her position and I learned to appreciate her more. From that time, I knew nothing would be easy in my life and I would have to look out for my education and myself.

Between grade school and junior high, the education I was given was mediocre. The public schools I attended taught the material but were not actually teaching. I realized by the end of the eighth grade that high school was going to be just the same and that I would have to push myself with my studies because if I did not, then no one else would care. During these years of my life I was struggling with my family. School to them was just a place for children to go during the day while they were working. Education was not an important factor in my family since no one in my family had ever finished high school. Especially since I was a girl, no one was pushing for me to continue into high school.

Before I continue I want to explain briefly that I am an Arab American, my religion is Islam and I am Muslim. There are many misconceptions about us and how we are. First and foremost I am not badmouthing my family. I am going to explain that coming from this cultural background and religion, the way the elders in my family perceived a woman's education was learning the basics of reading and writing. The elders consist of four main people, my father's uncle, who was the oldest, and his wife, my grandfather and grandmother. They were the oldest in our family and they were the ones who made the final decisions. My father's uncle and my grandfather came to this country always dressed formally, wearing dress shoes and suits. I remember that being seen always dressed nicely gave them a sense of authority, which is why we as children and my father and his brothers probably did not think to disrespect them. Their wives came to this country dressed in cultural attire, from what I was told. Though over time their clothing modernized, but their state of mind did not. My focus was to teach them to understand that having an education was important, and it would take a person further in life than owning his own mediocre business. Being a girl and continuing my education was my struggle.

Attending a low class high school in a bad neighborhood also worried my family, since I now started to become more independent, going to school on my own and learning to fend for myself. The elders were not too happy and began to notice that I had an interest in learning and wanted to further my education. After my freshmen and sophomore year things became more difficult. During this time my entire family and I were still living together in the same house. There was no privacy and everyone knew each other's business. Religion is not a factor here. Old cultural ways were the issue. According to the religion of Islam a woman has more rights than people assume. Women are allowed to work, learn, and be independent just like men. But culturally, people make up their own rule, which causes ignorant misconceptions of the Muslim woman. I love my religion and my faith. The elders in my family were the ones who made decisions and everyone else had to follow. Due to this I was always discouraged and was continuously told I did not need school, and that school was not important for a girl. The elders preached this because they thought women would not get far with an education.

I was not going to be discouraged any longer. My parents always supported me and were proud of me. They were proud because I was setting an example to the rest of my family. At this point, toward the end of my junior year, my father was becoming stressed from all the issues in the family. My father was the oldest of his siblings. He is an average height man with broad shoulders and dark hair and of course he was called upon whenever there was a problem, and he needed to resolve it alone. I realized at that time if I wanted to get further in my life with an education, my father had to take a stand as well. Living with everyone in one house is not easy and it made it difficult for anyone to be independent. Like my mother, my father had a lot to deal with as well. Being the oldest is very difficult for him. Moreover, the issues that my father was facing were similar to what I have been facing. To further my education I could not be around people who keep suggesting that I should not. The biggest step I ever took in my life was standing up to the elders with my father and moving out with my mother and siblings. I was sixteen and for the first time I felt like I could breathe on my own, not having negative people around me, telling me that I will not or cannot do something. This was the best feeling ever.

Moving from a predominately bad neighborhood to a very suburban neighborhood felt like culture shock. Coming from my previous high school and being the only white person in class to a school where I was not the only one was very different. The biggest difference I noticed was with the education at Susan E. Wagner High School. It was a public high school just like the previous one I attended, but the difference was that the teachers actually cared about the students. Being a student there, if you were attentive in class and wanted to learn, and asked for help, you were given that attention. I was given the opportunity to learn there. I was not at the top of my class and I was not great at every subject, though I had an interest in history. I seemed to be fairly good in my global studies classes and I tried my best. I liked learning about the past, past cultural history and American history. Ironically I enjoyed learning about the past world history yet I wanted to block out my own past. I did not want to feel that I couldn't do anything and that I wouldn't get far in my education, so I tried to not think about what had discouraged me in my past. I completed my senior year of high school and graduated. The feeling of accomplishment and believing in myself were the biggest steps in my life. After high school my next obvious move was college.

The summer before I began my college education I decided to visit the country my family came from. I am considered third generation living here in America and I needed to understand more about my family and myself. My great grandparents and grandparents came to America after the 1948 Arab-Israeli War for Independence, which was a civil war involving the British Mandate for Palestine between the Jewish Yeshiva force and the Palestinian Arab force in response to the UN Partition Plan. The State of Israel was declared. Then the Israelis took over the Palestinian side. This is still an ongoing issue in the world today and it goes as far back to biblical times as well. For me to understand my family better I had to go and experience it for myself.

Going to Palestine was the third biggest step I have taken in my life. I already had some knowledge about the issues, but seeing them with my own eyes was the biggest wake up call for me. While there I visited many people who knew my family and I stayed with different family members of mine who remained there after 1948. I will not get into the issues of the Arab-Israeli conflict but I will say that after visiting the country and seeing what I saw, and learning what I learned, I knew I must further my education in this life and make myself a better person, so that I can develop a better understanding about this world and the people in it.

My great grandparents and grandparents did not want to stay in Palestine because of what was going on and they knew that they would have a better life if they left. The reason why education was not so important to them was because they never had a chance for an education. They were put to work at a very young age and all they knew was to work for yourself or work for others. The women were taking care of the home and the men were taking care of the family. This was why school and education were not a factor. Because they never had a chance or anyone to push them to an education is why they see it as not a big deal. They were not pushed into school and had no encouragement, but if they had had the opportunity I believe they could have succeed and done very well for themselves. They only knew what their parents taught them about life and how to get by in this life. Culture was the issue in their lives as well as mine. They keep living in the past while we are trying to move into the future. It was motivating to visit Palestine and learn about its culture and ways. It gave me a better understanding about myself and who I am.

Beginning my college life was the next step in my education. I enjoyed taking different classes and figuring out what I wanted to do. When I knew I wanted to major in history, I was in for a rude awakening. Throughout my educational life, I had never encountered criticism from a person who was not a family member. My history classes were a place where I was able to learn about what I wanted and write about what I learned. I learned to form questions, how to write a thesis and research facts. This taught me how to think about the past and analyze what happened and why it happened. When learning that, I understood it was about decisions, the decision to go left or right, up or down. Whatever the case may be it is important to think clearly and analyze a situation. There was a point in my college education where I began to get ripped apart by a professor, a professor who I will not name but will be referred as Professor Q. In Professor Q's class we were given assignments each week that were short papers on various readings. After my getting my first paper back I thought a murder had been committed on my paper. I have never had a professor rip apart a work I had written so badly. I was literally told I should not be writing and I clearly did not understand history. After being criticized by my own flesh and blood, there was no way I would let this person talk down to me about my work.

For the entire semester I had to go through this class knowing that everything I wrote would be coming back in red. At the end of this class I had to write an important paper that would reflect on me as a historian. After this class I had to understand that I shouldn't strive just for an A, but I should try finish and be satisfied with what I was taught and how I could use it in my future. Although this Professor was harsh I took her criticism to my advantage and learned to be a better historian. Most of all I was taught to be a better writer. This was not the last time I had to encounter a professor like that, but I would rather be criticized about my work than being criticized as a person. I appreciate that I was able to take criticism well, for the reason that my own family doubted me and did not even want me to continue but I did. I appreciate my mediocre grade school education because I know better now and I don't regret any of it. The obstacles that I had to overcome may seem small to the reader but they were very big in my eyes. I had to learn to decide what was best for myself and what I wanted to do.

Being the only person in my family who has gotten this far with education is the fourth biggest step so far in my life. How I view my education now is still undefined, because I am still learning and it is just the beginning for me. My mother is a strong person and a very important person in my life. I look at my education and I observe how I think and analyze certain things, whether an assignment or an everyday life situation. It is of course different from how other people in my family think. My mother being the beautiful person she is thinks with her heart, and this is a special factor that not many people have. My mother loves my father so the task of taking care of a full house was thought out from her heart. It was a big responsibility and if I were in that situation I would think logically not emotionally. Although my mother never finished school and stopped at the ninth grade as well as getting married young, I know she is a very intelligent woman. She is the person whom I still learn from today because she has a different view of life. After we moved out on our own my mother taught herself to read and write another language. I took three years of a language and still do not speak a word of it. I encouraged her to continue this and get her GED but she believes that she is better off teaching herself and I envy her. All my life I fought to continue my education and go on to college and she taught herself and tutors children with math and English, as well as volunteering in many youth programs such as the Muslim American Society (MAS) I compare my education to my mother's self-education and know that she is just as smart as I am. She has developed in many ways and taught herself and continues to teach herself.

Furthermore, I found it interesting how Henry Adams speaks about his life and how he was taught certain things in his life. The way he defines his education reflects his outlook on life. Adams explains how his formal education was something diminutive and he believes that what his father taught him was more compelling than what he was taught in formal school. Adams believes that personal experience in certain situations helps a person develop in life. I believe this as well from my own experiences from visiting a different country and taking the experience into my everyday life. Although Adams attended a very prestigious Ivy League university he still thought he had learned nothing. At the end of his Harvard education he explained that while he was graduating, his education hadn't begun yet. Though he had learned many things, in reality he knew nothing. I believe this is true. In my life I have experienced many obstacles that I had to overcome and they only made me a stronger person. I am at the end of my undergraduate education and I believe I have learned a lot but I truly know nothing. Yes, I may know how to write and understand history but what does this mean? I still encounter new things in my life that I learn from.

The most important thing to me was teaching my family that education is important and that I am still learning.

As for CUNY and CSI . . .

The CUNY system has given Zana a great opportunity to have a college education. The College of Staten Island has some faults in her experience due to faculty and staff though she was able to look past that. CSI and CUNY helped her reach her goal and more, with the choices of classes to choose from as well as the help of certain professors. The educational range of students at CSI is vast, and there are students there who are not eager to learn or to be there. The difference is that Zana was able to see how CSI helped her become a better student so that she would always want to know more.

Although the CUNY system may have its flaws, a lot depends on how a person can fight through them. Her experience at the College of Staten Island gave her insights on what is to come in furthering her education. The professors she had the privilege of studying with taught her valuable information that she can take with her. The professors in CUNY are extremely underestimated and most have graduated from Ivy League colleges and have Ph.Ds. The downside to this is that Zana has come to realize that although they come from prestigious schools most of the professors are hit or miss. Either they are extremely knowledgeable, want to teach and also care about the subject matter. Or they are extremely knowledgeable and extremely arrogant, two very dangerous factors but again if you are a person like Zana you can find ways to look past this and continue at your pace and prove those professors wrong. At the end, however, Zana Ismail is at the end of her undergraduate degree and will be graduating with a Bachelor in History as well as minoring in Political Science and this would not have been possible if the College of Staten Island or the CUNY system were not there.

Z.I.

ZANA'S CLASSMATES RESPOND

"And knew if she can do it then no one can stand in her way." That was very inspirational to me because in my life I always let people's opinions take priority over my own happiness.

Zana is a warrior when it comes to education. It was not expected of her to go to college but she felt that it was important for her to do so. She states "The reason Zana was not able to fall into the traditional ways of her family was because she believed she was capable of much more." I believe Zana has tremendous capabilities. She did not let tradition get in her way. She believed in her abilities to gain a degree. Zana is making a statement, let no tradition stop you, let no one limit you, and pursue your dreams.

Zana, I find your discussion of culture to be very intriguing. People are profoundly affected by culture in many ways that can be both very obvious and very subtle. I admire your openness about your issues with your culture as well as your dedication to your faith. I think it is important for people to realize that having a purposeful relationship with one's culture, heritage and religion does not make one "backward," or "fundamentalist," rather it shows that that person is knowledgeable about their history and willing to embrace it as a part of what makes one who one is. One of the foremost reasons I have come to appreciate CSI is for its cultural diversity as it has helped to expose me to intelligent and not so intelligent, kind and less than kind people of many different backgrounds, who have provided me with many new and different perspectives on the world. Thank you for being one of them. (A nice and intelligent one, that is.)

CHAPTER 7:

GABRIELLA LEONE

"Shoot for the stars and if you fall short, you'll land among the clouds," said Dominick Leone to his daughter, Gabriella, as they discussed what she might want to do when she grew up. It was a motto he often repeated. He meant that Gabriella should set high goals so that if she achieved them she would be a "star" and if she did not she would still be better off than she was when she started.

Thus, at the age of ten Gabriella was certain she was going to get a full scholarship to high school and then to an Ivy League college, graduate with honors, get a law degree from Harvard or Yale and become a justice on the Supreme Court – if, of course, she was not elected to be the first female president of the United States. The first part was easy. When she was thirteen, Gabriella received a full-scholarship to her first choice, St. Joseph by the Sea High School. Her father was not there to see this accomplishment because he had passed away the previous year. Gabriella missed him terribly, but she knew he would be proud of her and would want her to continue to succeed and so she carried on with the plan.

Gabriella's years in high school, although stressful at times, were as wonderful as she had expected. She kept her scholarship and spent her entire four years in the honors program surrounded by peers who thought on her level and challenged her to do her best work. As those four years were coming to an end, Gabriella began to think about college. Junior year of high school, one of Gabriella's favorite teachers, Mr. Franz, handed out a poem by John Masefield, former poet laureate of Great Britain, in which he wrote, "There are few earthly things more beautiful than a university, a place where those who hate ignorance may strive to know, where those who perceive truth may strive to make others see." Mr. Franz told her and her classmates to make sure they picked a college that could foster their talents and make them feel the same way about college as John Masefield. Gabriella was nervous about this new imperative. While she still thought she wanted to be a lawyer, the chance of her getting into an Ivy League school seemed slim. She would go on to graduate fourth in her class, but Ivy League schools seemed to be looking for Valedictorians. Further, money was tight at home and Gabriella did not consider going into debt for an undergraduate degree to be an option. Thus, she adjusted her focus to the other part of her original plan – to a get a full scholarship to college.

Right before she began filling out college applications, Gabriella heard about the Macaulay Honors College, an honors program within CUNY, which offered students a full scholarship, a free laptop, a grant to fund study abroad or other learning experiences, and contacts with many competitive internships and employers. Macaulay sounded like the answer to Gabriella's college prayers. She would spend her four years of college among other honors students – just like high school. She was positive that her peers would "hate ignorance and strive to know" just as much as she did. Thus, she applied and was accepted.

Gabriella's perceptions were almost all correct. She did meet wonderful classmates who have challenged her to work hard and think harder – to speak up, become involved and influence change. However, unlike high school, Gabriella did not take all of her classes with honors students – only Macaulay's required classes. Thus, most of Gabriella's other academic experiences at the College of Staten Island have found her in classes with students who do not have the same academic skill level as Gabriella. Professors, then, have taught these classes at a lower level in order to help the other students learn concepts and skills that Gabriella learned in high school. In the following paper, one can read Gabriella's overall assessment of her education and understand her perspective about what the College of Staten Island and the larger education system are doing wrong.

G.L.

BEING SCHOOLED: THE EDUCATION OF GABRIELLA LEONE

According to the College of Staten Island, the goal of a college education is "to develop foundations for life-long learning, promote engagement with important local and global issues, and foster intellectual knowledge, practical skills, and ethical judgment."[2] Although these goals are noble, the policy is ludicrous. Students should begin to learn these "life-long" intellectual skills long before they reach college after twenty years of their lives. Unfortunately, this is the reality for many students entering college. According to a New York Times article, published last year, "Overall, 74 percent of city high school graduates enrolled at [CUNY]'s six community colleges take remediation in at least one subject."[3] This points to a failing public education system that is not even capable of producing competent readers or writers in its high school graduates. Such statistics might also suggest that the average student does not receive sound intellectual reinforcement at home. Resulting from these sad realities are the aforementioned flawed, educational goals of the College of Staten Island and surely many other colleges throughout the United States. To make up for the early-learning deficit, colleges are focused on building the foundation of intellectual thought when they should be finishing the roof.

Being the product of loving, supportive and involved parents as well as Catholic elementary and high school education – separate from the general public school classroom – I consider myself an exception to the bleak norm discussed above. When I came to college I had a passable "knowledge of the physical and natural world," thanks to my high school science classes. I was proficient in "critical and creative thinking" and "written and oral communication." I had a satisfactory "knowledge of quantitative and mathematical reasoning" and a comfortable "information and technological literacy."

[2] College of Staten Island General Education Committee, "CSI General Education Goals," (resolution, College of Staten Island, 2011).

[3] Michael Winerip, "In College, Working Hard to Learn High School Material," New York Times, sec. Education, October 23, 2011.

Finally, I possessed a well-developed sense of myself and my moral philosophy, as well as an experienced desire for "social responsibility and civic engagement." In short, I plan to show in this essay that I was reasonably far along in reaching the goals, quoted above, which the General Education Committee of the College of Staten Island set for students, before I came to college.[4] Thus, exempting a few experiences, which expanded my writing abilities, and my understanding of diverse populations and professional ethics, my college experience has been redundant and at times frankly futile. Despite this, the journey to my current academic position as a history major with the intention of teaching high school has been long, rich, and fruitful.

I believe my affinity for learning came from my talent for listening to and retaining information, which I have had since I was a child. Since my parents were older when they had me, I was often the only child at family functions; thus, I spent much time sitting at the dinner table with the adults and listening to conversation. In this way I learned how to become involved in polite conversation and express myself clearly and meaningfully. Indeed, my first word as an infant was "hi," which is still one of my most used words.

Outside of family functions, my parents often read and conversed with me when I was little and so I developed a respectable vocabulary and always excelled on standardized tests of reading and writing skills. My elementary school emphasized these types of skills and so we read Shakespeare in fifth grade and by the time I went to high school I had a firm grasp of the concepts of English grammar and syntax. This in-depth analysis of the inner workings of language fascinated me from the time my sixth grade teacher taught my class to sing a list of prepositions to the tune of "The Battle Hymn of the Republic," which I still remember. Language is still one of my favorite subjects to explore.

Because I received a full scholarship to high school, I was required to take two years of French and three years of Latin. Having never taken a

[4] College of Staten Island General Education Committee, "CSI General Education Goals," (resolution, College of Staten Island, 2011).

foreign language before, learning two at once was challenging but rewarding. Although I did not enjoy French, it taught me much about how the modern romance languages are structured. I liked Latin very much and wound up receiving the Latin award at my high school graduation. I also took one year of German, which helped me to get a better understanding of the development of the English language as well as how languages work in general. In college, I finally had the opportunity to study Italian, which I am currently doing. I have found that exposure to many different languages has made me a sharper thinker and a more precise writer because I have a thorough understanding of grammar and syntax. This is especially true of my experience with Latin and German because meaning in those languages depends on the endings attached to individual words instead of word order. Thus, in order to read German or Latin, one must have a clear understanding of what each word is doing in the sentence.

All of these experiences with language made me a stronger writer, an invaluable skill for a History major, but a class that I thought was particularly helpful in my development as a writer was English 151, which I took in my freshman year of college. Professor Paul Muhlhauser taught a special section of the course exclusively for students of the Macaulay Honors College. He approached writing from the point of view of a rhetorician and we discussed many vital concepts, including structures and approaches to an academic argument, parsing others' arguments to find their frame of reference and point of view and fallacies that invalidate arguments, just to name a few. Our final assignment for the class was to put together a portfolio of two drafts each of two of our papers from the semester, along with peer reviews we found particularly helpful. We were also to write a preface to the portfolio explaining our choices and what we had taken from the class as a whole. I wrote the following about my semester in English 151:

"I have gained a perspective on the surrounding world and the knowledge that one should almost never take means of communication at face value. I have learned to always search for the deeper meaning, think critically and find connections that I never before would have perceived. I have a long way to go before I can say that I am a 'rhetorician;' however, I am certainly on my way."[5]

Although I have not necessarily pursued my development into a "rhetorician" further, I took a lot away from the class in terms of the way in which I think about argument and motives behind rhetoric. This insight can only benefit me in my future attempts to teach my students to understand the events of the past from various perspectives.

My intention to teach high school history can be split into three main aspects: respect, propensity and interest. First, Oprah Winfrey used to say that teachers are her favorite people. Although there are some issues upon which Oprah and I differ, this is not one of them. Some of the people I most respect and admire have been teachers of mine. These individuals are highly intelligent, knowledgeable about their fields of study, compassionate and unflagging in their commitment to their students. Thus, it is my aspiration to carry on this tradition of excellence as an educator and be to my students the type of role model that my favorite teachers were to me. Second, I have always had a propensity for teaching. When I was younger, I often excelled in my classes and was able explain the material to friends who did not understand it as quickly. Later, in High School and College, I was able to take on a more formal role of "teacher" through the opportunities I have had to be a tutor. These have often required me to create informal lesson plans, think about how to comprehend subject matter from multiple perspectives and deal with students who learn in various ways at different paces. I find these tasks to be both challenging and rewarding and thus I am convinced that I could excel within the teaching profession.

Finally, my reason for wanting to teach Social Studies is simple. I am fascinated by the subject matter.

I suspect my love of history has roots in my childhood as well. I was always enthralled by the stories my parents told about our own family's history and my grandparents' immigration experiences from Italy. I thoroughly enjoyed going to museums when I was a child. I was fascinated with the ancient Egyptians and made my parents buy me many a book

[5] Gabriella Leone, "Portfolio," (paper, private collection, 2010), 7.

about mummies, especially King Tut. One of my favorite local attractions was and still is Historic Richmondtown, the reconstructed colonial settlement on Staten Island. I loved to go and interact with the actors in period dress and I always felt like I was being transported to another time. Along with English courses, I always excelled in my history classes in elementary school. I was engrossed in the stories of the past and even brought home my textbook for recreational reading once or twice.

Once I got to high school, I became utterly fascinated with Global History. My teacher, Mr. George Conlon, is one of the most knowledgeable people I have ever met. His lessons transported students through space and time to far-off countries and amidst global conflicts. I attribute much of my passion for and knowledge of Global History to Mr. Conlon and I only hope that I can emulate him in my own teaching career. I also enjoyed my course in AP American history, taught by another skilled and dedicated educator, Mr. Charles Abruzzo. My three years of Latin, were accompanied by a detailed study of Roman history, which culminated in my trip to Rome and Pompeii with my mother after I graduated high school. Seeing the ruins, which I studied for three whole years, in person was one of the most significant events of my life. Finally, my course in Church History taught me the story of my faith and sparked an interest, which I still pursue today. In fact, I wrote a paper, for a college history class, which I will discuss later, about the Jesuit missionaries in China because we briefly covered them in this class. It is worth mentioning that my Church History teacher, Mr. Christopher Franz, is another amazing teacher and even more wonderful person. He is almost definitely the most intelligent person I have ever met and one of the kindest as well.

The strengths and interests, which I developed in my high school history classes, have greatly influenced the classes I have chosen to take in college. For example, I enjoyed HST 220: Medieval Thought, which was basically a review of my Church History curriculum, including "Just War Theory," about which I wrote a paper for the class.[6] Another class I was

[6] Gabriella Leone, "Question #5: An Analysis of the Christian Theories of Just War and Holy War," (paper, private collection, 2010).

pleasantly surprised about was HST 327: Late Imperial China, which was taught by Professor Richard Lufrano, who is an impressive lecturer and possesses remarkable knowledge of his subject matter. He is definitely one of my favorite professors at the college and his class was one of my favorites as well. For Late Imperial China, or Early Modern China, as Professor Lufrano would prefer me to call it, I wrote a paper of which I am very proud about Fr. Matteo Ricci and his Jesuit Missions in China.[7] Finally, last semester, I took HST 300: Historiography with Professor Haj. The discussions in the class were always captivating and I learned much about the philosophy behind the methods of historical analysis, which I really liked. In fact, I am hoping to write my honors thesis by expanding the final paper I wrote for that class, which was a historiographical analysis of several historians' articles through the lens of Derrida's work on language and binary oppositions.[8] While these classes were interesting, I am not convinced that they taught me everything I need to know in order to be a successful history teacher. I had hoped that, by coming to college, I would gain new perspectives on the events of the past and their relation to the contemporary state of affairs, but that has not been the case. As I said, some of their content simply repeated what I learned in high school and the rest, while interesting, did not greatly increase my practical, factual knowledge of history.

Further, although most of my classes in the history department were pleasant, I have had some less than ideal experiences as well. My experience trying to write a research paper for HST 200: Historical Methods, which was possibly the most uninteresting and simplistic class I have ever taken, along with my time as a research assistant to a professor in the department were stressful and fruitless.[9] I discovered that while I am excited by the idea of holding primary sources in my hand, the process of searching them

---

[7] Gabriella Leone, "A Literary Friendship: The Story of the Jesuits in China," (paper, private collection, 2011).

[8] Gabriella Leone, "Listening for Silences: An Analysis of the Use of Deconstruction in the Historical Method," (paper, private collection, 2011).

[9] Gabriella Leone, "Staten Island Pride and the Road to Secession," (paper, private collection, 2010).

out and using them to write history frustrates me. These two experiences taught me that I would be much happier pursuing my career as a teacher than writing history for a living.

Similar to history and language, my sense of responsibility for leadership and civic engagement has flourished long before I set foot in college. I have always felt it necessary to be actively involved in the communities to which I belong. In my last year of elementary school, I joined my parish teen club and became a counselor at the annual Bible camp. In high school, I co-founded a peer-tutoring group and became Vice-President of the National Honor Society. Thus, when I came to college, it was my aim to become involved in the campus community. Currently, I am active at the College of Staten Island in several ways. I am involved in college governance as a student representative on the College Council as well as a member of the Academic Affairs and Student Bill of Rights Commissions on Student Government. While sitting on these commissions I drafted the Student Government Association's response to the Pathways Initiative – the City University of New York's attempt to impose a common core curriculum on all the colleges that belong to it by simplifying a curriculum that is already lacking in intricacy.[10] I am also an editor of and lobbyist for the Student Bill of Rights, which, if passed as a policy, will help to make students more aware of their rights and hopefully empower them to become more involved in their education.[11] I also work as a history and writing tutor in the college's Center for Academic Support in the Library two days a week. Finally, after I joined my parish's teen club in eighth grade, I never left. I currently coordinate the group with a childhood friend and fellow alumnus of St. Charles elementary school and St. Joseph by the Sea high school.

It is clear, then, that my own personal morality is closely linked with that of my Catholic faith, which my parents fostered when I was little and which I learned in greater detail throughout my years in Catholic school.

[10] College of Staten Island Student Government Association, "Resolution on the Pathways to Degree Completion Initiative," (resolution, College of Staten Island, 2011).
[11] College of Staten Island Student Government Association Student Bill of Rights Committee, "Student Bill of Rights," (resolution, College of Staten Island, 2011).

Thus, I am vehemently pro-life and I try to go to the March for Life in Washington D.C. every January. I have found that secular ethics operate somewhat differently than my familiar Catholic morality in that they focus more on professional duties than personal mandates. While I am resolved to operate according to the mandates set forth by secular ethics in my profession, they are, at times, at odds with my own Catholic morality in which case I choose the Church's directives as models for my choices. Despite this, I have found that college classes, such as Introduction to Ethics, The Peopling of New York (a Macaulay Honors College seminar), where we were required to conduct interviews for a website we put together on the ethnic diversity of Staten Island, Educational Psychology and my historiography class have helped me to understand the system of ethics that I must follow as a historian and a teacher.[12]

Another aspect of my personal development has been my interaction with varied groups of people. I have worked as a secretary at St. Charles' rectory for seven years. This has given me the opportunity to develop skills for communication with many different kinds of people - rich, poor, healthy, ailing, young or old - that the church serves. At the same time, having attended Catholic school on the south shore of Staten Island all my life, a large majority of my peers were of European descent – most often Italian, like me. My first interactions with people of another culture or faith came through my continuing friendship with two sisters who live next door to me and are Jewish. When my parents got divorced, my father married a Catholic convert from Judaism and so I learned a great deal more about the faith through her family and even attended their Hanukkah, Passover and Rosh Hashanah celebrations, of which I have only fond memories. My first experiences in a truly diverse environment, however, only occurred with my attendance at the College of Staten Island.

Indeed, Henry Adams writes of Harvard College, "It taught little, and that little ill, but it left the mind open, free from bias, ignorant of facts,

[12] Macaulay Honors College, "Staten Island." Last modified May, 2010. Accessed February 20, 2012. http://macaulay.cuny.edu/seminars/lavender10/index.php/Main_Page.

but docile."[13] I immediately related to this phrase when I read it because it successfully sums up my college experience as well. College has opened my mind to many different points of view. It has given me the opportunity to interact with a diverse population and learn more about individual cultures and ideologies and points of view that sometimes differ greatly from my own. I have made great friends, who inspire me to strive for academic and personal success and challenge me to effect change whenever and wherever I can. However, I do not attribute many of these gains to the academic programs at the College of Staten Island, but rather to the simple act of being on campus. Some days, I feel like my work in college governance has taught me more practical skills than all my classes combined. In other words, while I have found some of my classes to be challenging, I have rarely lacked confidence that I could ultimately succeed. My confidence does falter; however, when I consider the usefulness of overcoming the challenges the class poses. I often ask myself whether writing yet another research paper or book review will do anything to greatly expand my knowledge or practical skills. I often doubt it. In short, while I have valued most of my time in formal education, I am ready and eager to dispense with my time as a student and enter a new, challenging, exciting world as a working adult, who will do almost all the rest of her learning in the world and not behind a computer. I only wish academia and I could have parted on better terms.

As for CSI and CUNY . . .

It would be easy to conclude that Gabriella's apparent disenchantment with her college experience has been caused by her attendance at an inferior institution. Since it is common among Staten Islanders to question the quality of an education at the College of Staten Island – honors students from the Island's high schools scoff at the idea of even applying as a last resort – such a

[13] Henry Adams, *The Education of Henry Adams*, (Boston: Massachusetts Historical Society, 2007), chap. 4.

conclusion would probably not be questioned. However, simply writing off CSI as substandard is an unfair generalization, which ignores many significant issues that contribute to its status a flawed component of a failing system.

First of all, as Gabriella points out at the beginning of her paper, the widespread need for incoming students to take remedial classes in order for CUNY to consider them prepared to work on a collegiate level speaks volumes about the current state of the public school system. New York's schools (while they are most likely not the only offenders) are failing to graduate students who are proficient in basic reading comprehension, writing and mathematical skills. This deficit is reflected largely in CUNY's pool of applicants because so many of them come from New York City's public schools. Thus, CUNY is performing one of its main functions – to provide affordable education to residents of the city, but it is not necessarily providing the highest quality education because it has to back track and teach basic skills that students do not learn in lower levels of schooling.

One might argue that CUNY's senior colleges are not obligated to provide this lower level instruction because they can require students who are unprepared to do remedial work at the University's community colleges until they are ready to keep up with more challenging coursework. While it seems that such requirements vary among CUNY's senior colleges, the situation at the College of Staten Island is somewhat unique. Since CSI is the only CUNY institution on Staten Island and efficient transportation to other CUNY colleges, especially community colleges, is lacking, CSI's policy is to act as both a community college and a senior college. While this dual role is noble, it does not do much to advance academic quality at the school. Even if students pass their remedial classes and "proficiency" exams, they are often barely, if at all, prepared for the level of critical thinking that a challenging college class should require. Thus, professors, who wish to be charitable and refrain from failing a majority of their students, often choose to lower their expectations for a given course. While this practice may help the average student at the moment, it does not benefit the more advanced students in the class and it diminishes the reputation of the college as a whole. It is true that some do argue that CSI's classes are difficult – indeed, many do require numerous hours of reading, writing and other forms of busy work – however, one should consider that quantity of work is not equal to quality, depth or breadth of knowledge and understanding. It is this discrepancy, which seems to have most frustrated Gabriella.

Just when one might think that finding a balance between helping students prepare for college level work and offering college-level work to those who are already prepared could not have gotten any more complicated, CUNY decided to introduce a new challenge to the mix – the Pathways to Degree Completion Initiative. While Pathways has the very benevolent goal of creating a more efficient system of credit transfer throughout the University by creating a "common core" for general education, it has the capability to cause more problems than it fixes. One of the primary concerns one must have with Pathways is its effect on an already flimsy academic quality. Firstly it threatens quality because in some colleges, CSI being one of them, it requires current four-credit general education courses to be reduced to three. Since it seems CSI's approach will be to try to replicate its current general education requirements with considerably fewer credits, this will most likely result in a curriculum with a mere shadow of the quality it currently poses. Considering the current issues with quality, discussed above, this is not a comforting thought. Secondly, since Pathways was imposed in a very short span of time, CUNY's colleges are in danger of devising haphazard plans for its enactment, such as CSI's aforementioned attempt to reconstruct the current general education curriculum with fewer credits.

In addition to the major issue of quality, Pathways has also wreaked havoc in the ability of the faculty, staff and administration in CUNY's colleges, CSI being a good example, to engage in a responsible, professional dialogue about governance, policy or curriculum. Indeed it has reduced meetings of CSI's college governance bodies to gatherings that lack productive discussion and abound with disciplinary partisanship and bickering over trivia. Instead of addressing this truly poor academic leadership decision from CUNY's administration with professional aptitude and innovative thought, the leaders of the college community have collapsed into bitter, chaotic hysteria.

The most distressing part of the Pathways debacle is, despite their dramatic reaction, the faculty, staff and administration of CSI are perfectly capable of coming up with a successful solution to the problems plaguing the school if

they put their minds to it. They are a highly qualified, professional group who will hopefully realize that if they cannot dismiss Pathways they can use it as an opportunity to embrace innovation and cast aside a nostalgic attachment to the old general education. Perhaps they will be able to turn a potentially catastrophic administrative directive into an answer to the existing quality concerns. Perhaps they will develop separate programs for remedial and advanced students so that all students will receive the instruction they need and reach their fullest potential. Perhaps they will finally enable CSI to throw off the stigma of being a subpar college and truly let it live up to its slogan of being "world class, right here."
G.L.

GABRIELLA'S CLASSMATES RESPOND

Gabriella has more than an elementary grasp of the difficulties facing the Pathways concept of CUNY. She expresses herself with confidence and critiques Pathways in an intelligent and focused approach; unfortunately the behemoth that is the administration in CUNY does not bode well for a constructive outcome, as Gabriella eloquently states. It was refreshing to finally hear a positive vote for Catholic education in Gabriella's essay, after hearing nothing but negatives. I feel elevated academically having shared this project with her.

I assume Ms. Leone is about 22 years old. I mention her age because she seems to have packaged a tremendous amount of formal, academic schooling in those years, accompanied by a prodigious amount of learning. Her description of the complexity and intricacy of those various courses gave me a dizzying headache. It is a good indication that she wants to seek balance in her life pursuits by stating at the end: "I am ready and eager to dispense with my time as a student and enter a new, challenging, exciting world as a working adult." Too much of anything can sometimes not be a good thing. It was a shame Ms. Leone could not have gone to an Ivy League School because she has all the qualifications. If you include the large amount of time she spends participating in various volunteer organizations, she has no spare time to relax and enjoy herself. I can only assume the time spent being involved in all these volunteer projects fills her life with the happiness it needs. I was very saddened to learn of her father's death when she was only 13 years old. Gabriella and her mother are two strong women.

You have definitely been through a lot but used your father as motivation to help you overcome your struggles as well as make him proud. Growing up I had taken eight years of French. Although it is a nice resume builder to know several languages I believe it is something school institutions could do away with. Rather than force the students to take foreign languages, just make it an elective.

Your studying of different languages is very impressive and shows that you can take on new challenges. I agree with your opinions on history majors and the curriculum.

I agree about writing papers. As a history major we get several of them every semester. Sometimes I believe that it would be beneficial to be tested, to make sure we have an understanding of a variety of topics as opposed to just learning a lot about one.

Gabriella can reach for the stars because anything is possible. I can understand the deep questions that you have written in your paper. You say "I often ask myself whether writing yet another research paper or book review will do anything to greatly expand my knowledge or practical skills. I often doubt it." It's understandable why you would have such an outlook at the end of your road in college. I'm pretty sure many could relate. You seem to have very high expectations. You have strived to achieve those expectations through hard work and dedication. Receiving a college degree is wonderful but the true degree is your own self- knowledge. That is the key of fulfilling those expectations. When the research papers are over, when college is finished all that stands is you and all the knowledge within you. Gabriella I believe you can fulfill whatever expectations you have, whatever goals you set and if being a teacher is one of those expectation I believe you will be a remarkable one. You definitely have a great gift of listening and hearing others out clearly.

Like Fred, I, too, was sad to read that your father had passed away. He seemed to be an influential man in your life. Your exposure to languages is quite impressive, especially Latin at an early age. Have you considered becoming n linguist? Linguists are very important to history and help offer yet another great perspective when analyzing or translating documents.

Gabriella you are a very intelligent person and I admire you. Knowing many languages is a great thing and I believe you will go very far in your life.

I agree with Gabriella's opinion on written paper assignments. Normally when I receive my syllabus at the beginning of a semester, the first thing I do is read the requirements for the final paper, because I dread it! I believe in papers in order to delve into a specific subject, and gain more knowledge. However, I think at times testing is better in making sure that a student has learned the subject of the class for the entire semester. I also agree with others, who said the Gabriella's father was a tremendous influence in her life, and she should be proud of the young woman that she has become.

CHAPTER 8:
OLIVIA PORCH

The walls of formal education are not hollow, they are very much alive. The walls capture the story of each student, the laughter, the tears, and the sacrifice. The walls echo the stories but are the educators listening? Do they hear the stories or the voices of each student? I would say some are listening while others are dormant. As I was asked to write about my educational experience I did not just think of myself but all those stories, all those voices that have not been heard. All those educators that have fallen into a deep slumber, my story was written for you. I have opened up my memory, my mind, my heart, my soul to express the problems of formal education. I have learned the power of words and the power of the pen. I understand why so many ancient civilizations wrote down as much as they could. They either wanted to impact the future or change an issue in the present. The Mustard Seed reaches beyond the walls of formal education into the world. Since I was given this opportunity by Professor Hearten who hears the stories that echo in and outside of formal education, I am able to be heard. My voice will be able to reach individuals and students that went through similar experiences in the educational system. Our voice will echo inside and outside of formal education. The great joy I receive from sharing my story is that our voice is no longer silenced by the dormant educator. Let the voices be their alarm clock. Let the alarm clock of their failure ring. Let them awaken with all of their senses allowing them to see the thoughts, the observations of past and present students.

The walls captured your stories but the reality is the walls cannot bring your stories to life. Yes, the walls echoed your stories but it is not enough. Those tall blocks of brick keep your stories confined to a limited educational community.

The walls of formal education are temporary. Break down these walls, leap over them. Student: read, write, live life but most of all make sure you go beyond the walls of formal education. Go beyond what is visible to you, what is expected of you and go beyond what people think of you, Go Beyond!
O.P.

THE MUSTARD SEED

Olivia is writing to the world. She is writing to the human race. She will not be discussing her whole life story. Rather she will discuss a piece of her life. The piece of her life that she will discuss is how she was affected by the educational system. The advice she gives to her generation when reading her story is, "Do not just look at my words, see them. Listen to the words and hear my voice. Think a thought of your own. Grow a knowledge that is original. Do not be afraid of acceptance but learn to accept yourself, learn to accept the flesh of your skin, the eyes and ears, nose, arms and legs. If you are someone who does not have one of these abilities do not worry because you are made differently. The truth is we were all made differently. A man may have all his senses but throughout his life he can still be blind and deaf. Many would ask why or how? It is because he knows not who or what he is. Scientists look and look for our purpose through the stars, through technology, but the truth is, the answers lie within ourselves. Generation awaken and do not believe in negative labels because humans are not objects. Humans are not machines but they are emotional, intelligent beings. Each human has his own identity and the educational systems structure strips man away from his own purpose. It robs man of his own intellect. My belief is that there is another sense besides the five we carry. This sense has never been taught to my generation. It has never even been spoken about in schools. The sense would bring out our own enlightenment. It would end all questions of self-doubt. So hear my voice, my own original thought and my story of an educational system that confined, controlled me for fifteen years of my life."

The journey of education was not what Olivia expected. When she was about eight years of age she was already questioning the meaning of education. Education seemed a blur or better yet a bore to Olivia. She would try so hard in school but trying was not good enough. The other children, she started to notice, were moving faster than her in reading, writing and math. This always frustrated the little girl and soon education would be nothing but an enemy. Junior High School came and the feelings she had about education did not change. She would struggle on tests such as the city wide exams. These exams would place a student into a rating of how far they have come or how behind they are. Olivia did not feel that those exams gave the feeling of success but a feeling of being so far behind. This feeling of being a failure would become a very deep part of Olivia's life. The thoughts of being inadequate would sink into her brain and the feelings of success or succeeding were just a mere fantasy.

The last year of High School, she realized that looking back at thirteen years of school, that she learned one thing. The one thing she learned was absolutely nothing in school. The thought of going to College would be a waste of her time. The intervention of her family and boyfriend pushed her into the college scene. The intervention helped Olivia go to college but the motivation for getting a degree was for her loved ones and not for herself. The college years began and so did the roller coaster ride of formal education.

College began the same as High School because Olivia's mind was young and not developed. She would never really reach for an A in classes because she was adapted to B's and C's. Olivia did not and could not see herself as a scholar. As college went into the sophomore year, the young lady decided to declare her major. The major she declared was History. The reason she choose history was not because of pure interest. Her reason for choosing history was because she knew she was not good at other subjects. Subjects such as Math, Science, and English always seemed foreign to her. After thirteen years of school she was afraid of these subjects. These subjects left no impact on Olivia's memory or life because she was never taught how to use them. History seemed like an escape away from all other subjects. Little did she know that history had so many requirements such as reading comprehension, stellar writing and memorization and the requirements would be Olivia's worst nightmare.

She started her major and met some wonderful professors. Some professors would give her wonderful grades and some would just barely pass her. For Olivia coming straight out of High School this was normal. Although she did have expectations to do better than the norm, she believed that it was impossible. Some professors barely passed her or failed her and never said words of discouragement until one professor in 2009. The class was history 300 and she was excited. Olivia did not think she would come this far in her major but she did. This gave her hope that maybe she is smart, that maybe she has what it takes to be a scholar. Then came along Professor Dispirit and she was great at teaching but grading was something different all together. She would give exams and hand out half the class F's and Olivia was one of the students receiving this grade. Olivia would ask herself "I was in history 200 and I was not handed out F's. I was not given grades like this. These are grades given to a student who does not even show up to class." Olivia was furious. Although she received final grades with an F and this was only twice, she was never given test grades with an F in College. Olivia felt this was a new low for her. She felt if these grades from this professor were true than what about all the professors who gave her outstanding grades, what about all the professors who paved the way for her to get to this level, are they all liars? Olivia felt betrayed but she did not know who betrayed her. One of her thoughts was, "The educational school system has failed me. Am I trying hard enough? Maybe this Professor does not like me or just maybe all these professors that I have had really were being nice and passing me to get me out of school." Whatever the case, she felt betrayed.

The class was given the midterm and Olivia had already received an F on the first exam in class. She prepared very well for the midterm. She always participated and missed not one class, she wrote notes and even referred to the text that the class was told to read at home. One week later the midterms were graded and she could not wait for her results. Professor Dispirit wrote on Olivia's exam it stated "need to talk after class" and in the back of her exam it had the letter F. So Olivia stood after class and was hoping that Professor Dispirit would tell her what to do to better herself. Professor Dispirit looked at Olivia with a serious glare, she said "Olivia you were one of my favorite students but your writing is terrible. You need help with writing and honestly I don't know how you are going to make it to history 401. Maybe you should change your major to something different." Olivia's face turned solid red, she burst into tears, her heart and spirit broken, her mind confused. She stood on campus crying in the little circle where the water fountain is at building 1P, terrified that she was useless in this world and not capable of doing anything. She called her boyfriend and best friend, Alex and said "I'm dropping out, all my life I know who I am and what I am and I am nobody." Alex insisted that Olivia not drop out and not change her major. He told her to continue and not let one professor discourage her.

Olivia listened to a certain extent. She went back to College the next semester, this time going to do nursing like her boyfriend. She really was missing history so much because she felt she was starting to excel. She knew that taking biology was just a mess and it was not for her. She could not drown out the remarks the Professor gave her and this led Olivia to drop all of her classes that semester.

One whole year she was out of school. This was the best thing that she had ever done. Olivia went to find herself. She went off to find her abilities, to think and to understand her purpose in life. This was the beginning of her education. She finally had time to think for once, not be told how to think. She was finally human and not an experiment, not a machine. She decided to open up the Bible and read it for herself, not just sit at a service and listen to the words of a pastor. She sat down and studied the Bible as Abraham Lincoln had. The passage that gave her answers for her troubles with education was Hebrews chapter 11 called the Heroes of Faith. The heroes are the men that believed they could do all things through God, Enoch, Abel, Moses and Noah. They all believed that they could do extraordinary things in the world with God. They used faith as their tool to remove doubt and not let anyone tell them who they are to become.

They were to listen to the voice of God that would instruct them to do many works. The line in the scripture that stood out to Olivia was "Now faith is the substance of things hoped for, the evidence of things not seen," Hebrews chapter 11 verse 1. She realized after reading this verse thirty times that this was the answer. She realized the lack of faith and hope in herself blinded her to her abilities. She came to the realization that education had blinded her, it had left her in bondage and finally she was being set free. The letter grades she received labeled her and marked her for fifteen years of her life. The capabilities she had, no teacher, no man could tell her. The evidence is that her abilities are visible only with her hope and faith. They cannot be brought out by man, no man or woman can bring out her abilities, her qualities. Through her faith of knowing that something is inside of her, that she has a God given purpose in life, she can very well become the historical scholar that Professor Dispirit declared she could not be. The self-realization experience had brought Olivia back to College, better than ever.

She went straight into the fall 2011 semester ready for all the material in her classes. She met a wonderful Professor who taught about China. She learned so much about China and the dynasties. He gave exams, the exams were fair but she did not do that well. She was excited to hear that the class was going to do a research paper. Olivia made sure she went to the professor for whatever help she needed. He looked at her paper and only noticed that her citations and ending needed to be revised. She was so happy she did not hear words of discouragement but of betterment. This professor was truly uplifting.

Then she had a Professor that elevated her to a new level of consciousness. His name was Professor Hearten. He was everything she thought a professor should be. The class was intriguing, intellectual, free spirited and competitive. The class was based on the Trial of Galileo. We were spilt into three teams the cardinals, the scientists and then people in the middle. The whole way through she remained a cardinal. She was happy because she truly believed in God. The first paper was a C and indeed it was not great but Olivia pushed even further and received A's. Her favorite paper is the second to last in the Darwin game when she played the cousin and friend of John Snow. She goes completely against the Malthus theory and she states, "Darwin's theory focuses too much on the ideas of Malthus. Malthus believes "That population increases more than the means of increasing subsistence does, so that in time, if no check is put upon the increase of population, many must starve or all be ill-fed. Applied to individual nations, like Britain, it suggested that something must be done to check the increase of population, as all the land would not suffice to feed its inhabitants." Adolphe Quetelet disputes the Malthus doctrine. He believed the law of error could be applied to human beings. Quetelet believed that it was possible to determine the average physical and intellectual features of a population. He believed it possible to identify the underlying regularities for both normal and abnormal behavior. Through statistics Quetelet shows that Malthus' mistake in his doctrine is probability in nature. Malthus does not think about intervention and saving life, preserving life but rather he used science in a more negative way only for misery and vice. Through statistics we are able to understand what goes on society, what works what doesn't, the behavior of races and nationalities. Malthus cannot prove that many people will starve. Who is to say people are selfish and won't share or care for the poor or working class? Malthus' doctrine is based on assumptions. My cousin John is proof that statistics saves lives and improves public health." She loved this quote from her paper because she truly believes in the human race. The human race does not have to look at the color of their skin or be blinded by their class status. She has much faith in the human race and its development. Every time she reads this passage she feels the human race is limitless. The only way the human race is limited is through their own minds, their own hearts, because they both are deceiving. This class gave an experience of a lifetime because it opened up her mind to research topics of the church and science.

Finally she knew it was time to take history 300. The time was destined, the professor was perfect and Olivia was ready. The Professor was a teaching adjunct but he seemed a lot wiser and smoother in his teaching style than most. The name she gave him was Professor Future because he was young; bright and was a professor who gave a hope for the future to come. The grades she received in history 300 were all great and she began to notice even more of her talents in history. Since she had Professor Hearten she decided in history 300 to do her massive paper on the Historical Jesus. Many in the class felt it would be difficult but it was not for the young lady because the Bible was her first education.

She found three historians and as a historian she put aside her own beliefs. She began to read the material objectively. The first historian was an atheist and he made it very clear that he was. He said there was no evidence for Jesus's existence on earth. The second historian explained that to leave Jesus in his own time and place is the only way to understand him. The third historian was an atheist but he had the best historical approach. He said he did not believe in the miracles. The miracles cannot be proven. He also believed that Jesus existed and there is no way anyone can deny it. In Olivia's last page of the paper she wrote "The most remarkable argument was from Grant. He was looking into the Text objectively. He was searching for the historical Jesus and did not give up. He made the most logical sense that Jesus was a man born into the world. That his life can be reconstructed and we must take out what is significant from that reconstruction. He believes it is hard but it is not impossible to find the historical Jesus. Grant strives to achieve this goal of finding the historical Jesus. The historical Jesus that Fredriksen describes could not be understood in the modern context because only his contemporaries could understand Jesus in his time and place. The historical Jesus Wells simply gives up on is because he has come to the historical documents with a narrow approach and presumptions. Grant is searching with an open-mind, travelling mentally into a time before his own and captures the historical Jesus." Olivia really started to notice she was developing as a historian. She put aside her religion. She put on the armor of historian, traveled outside of her comfort zone and began to learn even more. This class pulled her into another world, the world of the historian. The History 300 class was better than the one she took a year before it was encouraging, uplifting and life changing as well.

The class Professor Dispirit said Olivia could not reach, she did. Olivia was amazed that she got up, shook off all the negative remarks from Professor Dispirit and found her own value, her own worth. She believes this was all part of a plan for her life God makes no mistakes. She was given a paper that she took to heart in history 401. The paper was on our education and whether it affected her in a positive or negative way. She also had to find someone that she could compare her education too.

The person she chose was Thomas A. Edison. This man produced over 1000 inventions. He believed that one should never be discouraged, to try and try again until one succeeds. Olivia sat down in the CSI library and read Thomas Edison's diary and sundry observations. As she started reading his diary she could not stop because his thoughts on education were similar to hers. She started to feel like she met him in another life. Everything he wrote was imprinted already in Olivia's mind and she believed it was fate that brought her to read his diary.

When Thomas Edison was young his appearance was fragile and he had a weird shaped head. Already Olivia and Edison had something in common. His mother overheard his school teacher call her son "addled." Edison's mind would often wander, so he was kicked out of school. His mother decided to teach him but at the age of twelve, Edison lost his hearing. He could hear, but very little. Books would become Edison's best friends. He would love books and he did not read just books, he read the whole library. Edison was self-educated. He was allowed to think and not be told how to think.

Thomas Edison made it very apparent that failure is just an opportunity for success. He was conducting an experiment and it did not succeed. His associate expressed discouragement. Edison writes "One of my associates, after we had conducted the crowning experiment and it proved a failure, expressed discouragement and disgust over our having failed "to find out anything." I cheerily assured him that we had learned something for we had learned for certainty that the thing couldn't be done that way, and that we would have to try some other way. We sometimes learn a lot from failures if we put into the effort the best thought and work we are capable of."[14] This statement that Thomas Edison makes cannot be taught in schools. One of his associates is crushed by failure while Edison is able to shake it off and accept the failure. Both men were working on the same experiment but they had two different views about failure. One can conclude that both men have very different life experiences. Olivia can only conclude from Edison that he saw the difference between himself and others. He saw that he was different and just because he was not accepted in a public school does not make him a failure. The failure is the fact the public school could not adapt to his needs. It could not understand his genius, because his thoughts often wandered since he was thinking past his school system into the future. Olivia, just like Edison, viewed failure as an opportunity to succeed. She realized one must accept failure, see the negative and turn it into a positive through hard work and dedication. It is true and Olivia knows every man has his own approach to failure and every individual is not the same when it comes to the recipe for success.

Thomas Edison spoke of the age of speed. He wrote about his thoughts on the educational system. He believed the world was moving fast: "This is the age of speed, speed such as men had never dreamed before. We are annihilating distance, we are conquering not only the land and sea but the air-we are doing what our grandfathers could not have done in days. They were not equipped mentally to grasp or utilize the new order of things which burst upon them"[15]. Edison believed that this age of speed was nothing good. He believed man could not grasp or use this new order of learning. He believes moving fast does not make one more intellectual. Moving and thinking at one's own pace would make him or her more intellectual.

Edison was questioned about the educational school system and his response was "I am frequently asked about our system of education. I say that we have none. Our system is a relic of past days. It consists of parrot-like

[14] Thomas Edison, *The Diary and Sundry Observations of Thomas Alva Edison*, (New York: Philosophical Library, 1948), 43.
[15] Edison, 107.

repetition."[16] This statement from Edison is exactly the way Olivia sees the educational system. She believes fully that the system does not help man conquer the future but allows man to sink into the past. It does not allow man to express his own thoughts but dictates to man only to accept the thoughts of past philosophers, scientist and scholars. The educational system only sticks to past routines which turn into tradition. Men were made to break tradition, break barriers and conquer the world the best he or she knew how. There is no education because education is hidden inside of an individual through life experiences, through his very human nature. The school system cannot adapt to every child but the child can learn to adapt to his or her own condition.

Olivia continued to read the diary of Edison and the thoughts Edison had on the educational system began to get deeper. She really started to think she and Edison were the only two children that felt the same about the school system. Olivia and a genius; how many more feel this way? Edison writes more on education. He states, "The trouble with our way of educating as generally followed is that it does not give elastically to the mind. It casts the brain into a mold. It insists that the child must accept. It does not encourage original thought or reasoning, and it lays more stress on memory than on observation."[17] Olivia began to shake her head. She was in total agreement. She could not think of a time in her early childhood education or secondary education where she was given time to think for herself. Education does cast the brain into a mold; it tries to develop the brain according to a standard. This standard is not human. The human condition before education was developed was for man to think for himself. What is in the best interest of the human race? The best interest is to think and observe the world around one. Edison says he holds the brain above the book. This quote stood with Olivia because in her generation how do we really approach our intellectual level? We approach our level of being intellectual through the books we have read. In classes we read and read to remember for an exam or a paper but we never truly observe the

[16] Edison, 111.
[17] Edison, 113.

quality of work. We never truly understand our interpretation of what was written. This is the art of learning, being able to read understand and adapt the material to one's life.

The most profound statement that Edison left Olivia with is prophetic and moving. He states, "It is clear to me that our schools and colleges are turning out men who not merely have failed to learn, but have been robbed of the capacity to learn."[18] Her generation would all shake their heads because in the media even the elite have said the educational system is a failure. The students are failing and they cannot understand why. So the elite conducts tests upon the newest school teachers to see if they pass or fail. Olivia starts to think and has a profound thought "These new teachers are part of my generation. The school system has been failing, so weren't these teachers once students? Weren't they a part of a failed system. They have been robbed of truly learning. They have been robbed of the true education, the education of themselves. They have walked around for years as zombies. They have never had their own identity. Olivia sees her generation looking into the mirror and not seeing who they truly are. Her generation continues to carry a heavy burden of grades and marks that have only left scars. Her generation also grows with the constant worry that if they do not receive an A they are not good enough. The marks or grades do not make an individual who he is and it never will.

The Diary and Sundry Observations of Thomas Alva Edison left Olivia speechless. She can admit she has had wonderful professors. She even mentions experiences with great professors but she believes those professors can teach because they have found themselves. They have had their own experience with self-realization. They have picked up books on their own time such as Thomas Edison did. They wanted to learn. They wanted to help and most of all they did not want to just succeed but they wanted to understand and learn of their own abilities. The educational system would be wonderful if many could have time to think on their own because those who think on their own are the best teachers. Those professors who fail half of the class do not question their own abilities. They do not know their

---

[18] Edison, 119.

own identity. They are only holding the book above the brain and they have become the failed educational system. Those teachers need to first teach themselves, not through a book but through their own God given brain. The teachers who perform the best believe in their student's abilities. Thomas Edison spoke of his mother who was an educator and stated "My mother was the making of me. She was so true, so sure of me, and I felt I had someone to live for, someone I must not disappoint."[19] Edison's mother is an example of what every teacher should be. The teacher should believe in a student, encourage and take the student to higher level of consciousness.

In the spring of 2012 Olivia has reached graduation. Hopefully, God willing, Olivia will be receiving her Bachelors in the month of May. She was not lying when she mentioned education was a roller coaster ride. She hit her highs and she hit her lows. The most life changing educational times amazingly were the lows. The lows brought Olivia into an awareness of herself. She would come to the realization that education does not define her but that she defines education. Education is natural. It is what makes human beings different from every living thing on earth. It is in our very nature to be intellectual. No one on this planet is disabled. No one on this planet is limited. Edison believed that Helen Keller was highly educated. Helen Keller was blind and deaf and still she was educated. Man has blinded themselves and deafened his own ears even when he physically has these abilities because he has no identity.

Whenever Olivia wakes up she is in a higher awareness like Thomas Edison, Albert Einstein, Abraham Lincoln, Walt Disney because they have all awoken from a century's slumber. She has risen to the level of understanding that nothing is wrong with her. That nothing is wrong with her whole generation but there is something terribly wrong with the educational system. She believes that every day, hopefully, someone is awakening from the century's slumber and eventually the time will come when man follows his own intuition, his own sixth sense, the sixth sense of being aware of his own competence.

---

[19] http://inventors.about.com/od/estartinventors/a/Thomas_Edison.htm

As for CUNY and CSI . . .

Dear America

I am writing to you with great concern. I want to change you. I want to help you when it comes to the educational system. I believe that College will not function properly or fulfill its purpose because elementary and secondary education have failed completely. I do not stand alone on my theory and it has been already proven years ago. The great Thomas Edison did an experiment that reveals the problems education has from elementary school leading up to college. Edison was beyond his times when he conducted this experiment. The experiment was done on college graduates to measure their intelligence and memory. He was an employer looking to hire, so he made a questionnaire for the college graduate. He put questions that a college graduate should know. He wanted to see if College works and the results he received were alarming. Edison states "I never before was so shocked and astonished as I was by the results. It is obvious that our schools and colleges are benefiting but a small proportion of those going to them. The experiment makes revelations with regard to American Education which are not less than appalling, with the college making a far better showing than the lower schools, although it is quite clear that even the colleges and institutions are far from what we fondly have been hoping them to be. The lower the schools the results seem to be tragic. Perhaps the failure of the colleges lies principally in their lack of appreciation of the dull inferiority of the material which the lower schools deliver them; it may be because of this that they do not go down the line to help toward the correction of national evil."[20] *This revelation that Edison reveals is speaking to us in the present, warning about the problems that can affect the future. How can college work if elementary and secondary education are broken? It does not work. Once the lower educational system fails the whole system fails, meaning college fails right along with it. How can any educational institution give grades if it is a failure in and of itself? The sad truth is even though it is a failure and*

[20] Edison, 130.

a national evil, the educational system continues to give grades and destroy lives. The Colleges should be trying to change the problems that they see in the educational system. I'm in agreement with Edison that the Colleges are so comfortable with the students coming to them already dumb so they do nothing to change elementary and secondary education. Remedial courses for me do not cut it. The remedial courses are a cover up. A student should go to college already knowing math, how to read and write. If the student goes to college not knowing math, how to read or write the student has been robbed by the educational system. They tell these students to take these remedial courses, pay for them and give them no credits toward their degree. Why should a student be paying for a damage done to them through the educational system? It is as if the student is blamed for problems that they did not create. When attending College the goal of the institution should be to bring out the abilities that the student and teachers of elementary and secondary education have already discovered. The writing, reading and math should be so high that the professors feel challenged by their students. CUNY institutions should be appalled and devastated that they even implemented remedial courses. Remedial should have been a temporary fix until professors and administrators of CUNY took care of the problem of secondary and elementary education. Since they have not fought against the problems of elementary and secondary education, the CUNY institution has joined the national evil.

I attend the College of Staten Island and it is a CUNY institution. The first positive thing I hear about CUNY is that it is affordable but in the past it was free. Affordable and free are two different things. Taking out loans that increase over time is not affordable. Students come out with debt from CUNY institutions and this is bad for middle class students. I was fortunate to receive financial aid but I do not just think of myself. There are students I hear that are one penny over the limit for getting financial aid so they have to take out loans. This is so upsetting not just for the student but for the family that is struggling. Also books are overpriced. If you go to the book store to get three books it can add up to your entire rent. This is a crime and a sin for any student to have pay two hundred dollars for one book. In the past books at CUNY institutions were less expensive. College education was free allowing no excuse why an individual cannot get a college education. Money has been more of a concern than the actual learning and education of the student. My question is, the CUNY institutions ask for money but is their education so good, so up to date with the modern world and society that they can ask for money? Absolutely not, they are behind. Some students sit down in the College library and teach themselves. I know. I work in the CSI Library as a college assistant. Many of the students I have spoken to say, "My Professor is from another country and I cannot understand a word that comes out his or her mouth, so I'm here at the library teaching all this material to myself. I hope I pass." These statements really make me think "why is this student even paying tuition at this institution if they are forced to teach themselves?" Money has become a big problem in CUNY institutions. If I was to save anything at the CUNY institutions it would be the library. The library has helped and rescued a lot of CUNY students. I've learned more working in the library of the college than as a student of the college.

The largest problem with the CUNY institution is grades, GPAs and professors. GPAs have absolutely no worth for proving an individual's intelligence. The 4.0 student is smart and so is the 2.0 student. I find that just because you have a 4.0 does not mean that you are far more intelligent than the 2.0 student. Students with 4.0s, do not get me wrong, you work hard for those grades. You stay up day and night. Some of you receive As naturally. The student that has a 2.0 most of the time focuses on certain subjects of interest. They feel like living more than sitting at a lecture. They are more visual learners. The 2.0 student believes in adventure. The student that has low grades but has high communication skills can deliver in America. This student cannot learn completely from textbooks; they must experience the journeys of history, English, math and science in life. The 4.0 student may feel he is a visual learner as well. This could be true but the 4.0 student who is a visual learner forces himself, stressfully, to get that A. Even though they do not like the educational process, they want desperately to get out of whatever financial problems they are in by using a CUNY institution. The problem that stems from this belief is that in the real world grades and GPAs from a CUNY institution do not matter. Sometimes what matters is who you know. The biggest problem for the 4.0 CUNY students is the SUNY student. When looking for a job most get turned down because SUNY students have a far more prestigious label attached to their name. I'm upset for that 4.0 CUNY student because he worked hard believing that education would change his live. CUNY forgot to send you the message that the 4.0 you carried most or all of college career means nothing in the real world. Most of these 4.0 students wind up working jobs that require high school diplomas. So do not just depend on the 4.0 GPA to carry you through in the world. Depend on your identity and what makes you different from all the rest, to show that you have abilities that the SUNY student does not have. This is why it is important not to let labels of grades and GPAs become who you are. That's why I said GPA's mean nothing; they just separate the student body from one another in a CUNY institution. In the real world the 4.0 CUNY students are looked at as equivalent to the 2.0 student in the SUNY institution. The 4.0 CUNY student starts to see the inequality that he faces being middle or underclass in society. Most just give up on job searching and compromise for any job that swings their way.

The grades of a CUNY student are based on subjective criteria. Some professors love your papers, while others think your papers are horrible. One says you cannot write, while the other professor says you can. This hurts the progress of a CUNY student or any student for that matter. Many professors have different ways of teaching, while students have different ways of learning. This is very problematic. The reason it is problematic is because your writing cannot evolve naturally and intellectually. The student starts to question the motives of each professor, whether the professor is just passing you by or the professor does not like your writing style. It is very complex for the student and it should not be. If every professor is doing his job at the CUNY institution you should never have to question your progress. America, if secondary and elementary education's problems were fixed no child would ask about their progress in College.

The question every student asks frequently in his mind or out loud to the teacher or professor is "How can I use math, science, history and English in real life?" This question is most of time unanswered by teachers and professors. The student winds up shying away from subjects when this question is left unanswered. The professor or teacher often can read from the text book about experiments.

They discuss in class others that have conducted experiments, but the truth is the teacher has never conducted his or her own experiment. It's as if a person tells you science is awesome. Than you ask "How it is awesome? How do you use science? How do you apply it to life?" The person answers, "Well it is just awesome, using science is easy you just read and learn about past scientists. How you apply it to life is easy, you just study hard and pass exams. If you pass these exams you understand and know science." This is a huge problem. Many professors and teachers have no idea what they are teaching. Every subject can be applied to life and how it's used in life. Professors in science should be conducting their very own experiments in the present. Professors in math should be showing how they built houses or domes from a mathematical equation. Professors in English should be making books that draw the attention of their students and people around the world, showing students how to bring out their thoughts and voices using a pen. Professors in history should be producing books based on the history of the modern world. They should not just be writing books about the past but of current events. They should be picking up where inventors, historians and other figures of history left off. The professors of history should be alive with discoveries to share to their students of their progress not just academically but in life. All professors, teachers of secondary and elementary education should be able to show examples of their present activities in their field of work. They should show how they use their subject matter in life, in the world. The best Professor I can use as an example is "Indiana Jones." Indiana Jones was a character in a movie but in real life History professors should be just like him. He does not just talk about his subject matter but lives and uses his subject matter in real life. His students can learn from him. Learning would come to life if professors knew how to use their subject matter in life. Textbooks are not enough. The student should come to the understanding that their teachers and professors have a well-rounded education. The professors and teachers have to go beyond the walls of formal education in order to affect their students in the classroom.

America,

I have encountered and watched others encounter the very problems with the educational system. I'm tired. In the fifteen years I went to school I could not wait to get out. Some of these professors and teachers are my peers or a little older, still they are part of this cycle. The cycle that robs all of us of learning from one another. No one is a winner in the educational system. Either you lost your identity through labels and grades as a student, or when you graduated you did not know how to apply the knowledge you learned to your actual life. You work at a job that has nothing to do with what you majored in. The professors or teachers have no clue how to teach or what they are teaching. The American student faces inequalities when he or she gets out of a CUNY institution and applies for jobs. The list is so long of the problems that formal education has that a person could write at least five books to explain them. It is truly a crime. A crime all of us are responsible for. If you are a student who encountered the problems within the educational system you are also responsible for the future of your countrymen. Running away as soon as you get out of school solves nothing. Running towards those problems to solve them makes not just America a better place but the world. So listen to my voice, my own original thought and the sole of my sneakers screeching fast toward the very doors that haunted me, running toward the educational system that robbed and controlled me, running to solve the educational crisis in America.

Sincerely yours
The Mustard Seed
Olivia Porch

OLIVIA'S CLASSMATES RESPOND

My first reaction to Olivia's introduction of "Beyond the Walls" was the 1970's Pink Floyd album of "The Wall." It goes like this, with the chorus sung by English school children: "We don't want no education, we don't want no thought control. Hey, teacher leave those kids alone. All in all, all you are is another brick in the wall." Olivia mostly talks about her experiences with the public education system in New York. Those experiences were disappointing and emotionally draining. It was only after experiencing the epiphany of a religious conversion that Olivia came to comprehend and inculcate into her belief system a comprehension of her societal status and affirmation of her own self-worth, or as she put it, "self-realization." I still don't understand why the educational system imbued her with such a toxic elixir of worthlessness and hostile self-alienation. The writing she does for her life essay contains an abundance of intellectual complexity and sophistication. Although Olivia talks about the educational experiences of today's twenty-somethings, unique to her generation, it is not a new phenomenon. All of humanity has been saying their educational system is dysfunctional, not meeting the needs of their students, for hundreds of years. This assessment, however, does not excuse, or rationalize away the plight of people like Olivia. It just sets up a condition of anger and frustration that is ad infinitum.

Once more, I want to thank Olivia for her care and concern for the future of her country. I suggest that you stay involved in an effort to change society. On my job with the city, I got involved in labor union politics. We did not always win, but we made a difference and sometimes changed things for the better. Best Regards.

Olivia and her negative experiences in education only helps enforce my firm belief in the adage: "if you can't say anything nice then don't say anything at all." Let's apply it to the delicate psyche of a child just starting out on the journey that is their education. They are so full of hope and limitless possibilities for the future, so how an educator can think he has some divine right to destroy these ideas in a child or even a young adult is beyond the scope of what I would consider an educator. I have heard all too often a teacher or professor tell a student that they were incapable of receiving their degree in a given field; let the students make these calls on their future, not an incompetent teacher. Perhaps if these students are dealt with fairly they themselves will come to the right conclusion for their future.

Over the course of this semester I kind of got to know you and I can honestly say I would have never thought that this professor (I don't like her either), would get to someone like you who has strong beliefs which are really thought out as well. We had discussed once in class how you plan on opening a school that focuses on a child's ability since everyone is good at a few things rather than many things and that the whole grade system really affects children especially when they get bad grades. You have some really good ideas and you should let them come to fruition.

I cannot believe that a professor had the audacity to recommend you change your major. Some people major in a topic for money, and others (like you) for the love of it. If a student is struggling and the professor realizes this, then he/she should be responsible for trying to help that student.

Wow, I cannot believe that way that professor made you feel or her comments that she made to you. You're a strong young women who fights for what she believes in and have come very far and excelled in your education. This story just shows how you should not let anyone discourage what you believe in or want to do. Good job!

This is a deep piece that highlights many ups and downs in Olivia's life. I am glad you were not disheartened by your negative professor's words and you were able to carry on. Perhaps you can look back on such a negative event in your life as a test or trial to yourself that you have overcome.

Even though this professor discouraged you to the extent that you felt like you had to leave school, you still came back full force and clearly proved her wrong. I hope she looks at this and realizes no one should be spoken down too no matter what. Also I believe you are a strong person to come back and finish what you started.

Olivia's essay shows that she is a fighter! Although she has had struggles in life, including one with a professor who was completely out of order, she persisted through them. This essay should be read by anyone trying to understand how the power of believing in yourself, and your ideas, can change not only your life but others!

CHAPTER 9:

ROSANNA SANTANGELO

Similar to the great Henry Adams, Rosanna was born into a family that could give her a formal education. Yet, in contrast to Henry Adams, Rosanna was not against receiving a formal education. Unlike Adams, Rosanna understood at an early age that she had a lot to learn in school. She was known to be "book smart" but not "street smart." This uninformed girl grew up believing that without a college degree, her life would be a waste of talent. She never considered taking her artistic talents seriously and she now wonders where she would have gone with that. Rosanna now believes that one should pursue a formal education but that does not mean that one will achieve full happiness and prosperity.
R. S.

A HISTORIAN'S INTRIGUING STORY

CHAPTER 1- MY INFLUENCES DETERMINED MY ACHIEVEMENTS

Many agree that a person's education can be influenced by another person's education; in my story, I am influenced by an uneducated person.

As early as Kindergarten, I was heavily influenced by my father to achieve the best education I could. My father was born and raised in Italy, and came to America with his parents and an older brother in his teen years. Because his parents did not value education, my father did not go to high school and started working by the age of thirteen. He would have jobs as a dishwasher in restaurants in Brooklyn, and a carriage driver in Central Park in Manhattan with my grandfather.

My father's only education was lessons in hard manual labor, and starting that at such a young age. He was taught trades that would later benefit him in the laborers union. The union he is in was what he considered a golden ticket for his life, because his dream was to take care of his family. My earliest memories were sitting at the dinner table listening to stories of his life and how hard he works to give me and my family a home and a comfortable living. He stressed the importance of education and how life changing it is to receive the best education I could.

At such an impressionable age, I believed everything my father told us, and what I would see for myself. My dad coming home every day, dirty and exhausted, I would be terrified that I would have the same future if I didn't do well on my tests in elementary school. He is major influence on my success in my education. He was the reason I was so smart in school, and every grade I completed at the top of my class.

I graduated St. Margaret Mary School as salutatorian and class president. I was a born leader, and it is because of my father, who gave me the determination to be so. Outside of school at that age, nothing else is important in your life besides your family. On holidays and family functions, I could sense as a child, the lack of respect my aunts and uncles showed towards my father, and I would hear the conversations between my parents about the way he was treated because he was uneducated and just a construction worker.

My father, since then until today, always talks about retiring, he hates what he does and the only purpose he has for being a construction worker, is for the money. Being so young, I didn't fully understand why he wouldn't just be what a fireman or a doctor if he wanted to, but I knew that it was because he missed his opportunity at a formal education, he couldn't do anything but what he was doing.

CHAPTER 2- THE REASONS FOR MY GOALS.

I decided before high school that what I wanted to do was become a lawyer, for numerous reasons. The most important reason was because I saw and felt the heartache my mother had when she was put through a heartbreaking lawsuit within her family that lasted years. I obviously did not fully understand that court system, but I did understand the nonsense that she was put through, and I wanted to change that for her and for anyone else put in her situation. Another reason being that by becoming a lawyer, I would gain the respect from others that my father never received.

In the eighth grade, I went to every open house to find a high school that I wanted to go to. In Catholic school, they undermined public education, and claimed that only Catholic high schools had the prestige to get a person accepted into a great college. Being in Catholic school, where you knew every teacher and student and every teacher and student knew you and your parents made it feel like a second home. However, each grade felt like a different challenge. Every teacher I had I believe did not meet the criteria of being a great teacher, or even a teacher at that.

It was in my later elementary grades that made me decide I wanted to become a teacher and I believe it was for all the right reasons. I have memories of being such a successful student and my teachers disliking me for it. My peers and I were all treated differently by our teachers. I have vivid memories of each teacher and what I learned from them. I remember my teachers more as how they were as teachers rather than what they taught me in my education.

Of the eight teachers, only one was unbiased and she was the Kindergarten teacher. Every time my feelings were hurt, I would take a mental note for myself on how to become the perfect teacher. As petty as it may sound, my teachers always favored the "cute" kids. From my vivid memories, I feel as though I graduated St. Margaret Mary's yesterday. And when I attended school, I can remember feeling like I was there longer than I was home. So, as a teacher I would make my students feel like I am their second mother, because they will be in my care for most of the day until their summer breaks. I would treat them as though they are my own children, with care, compassion and respect.

My teachers would also get very agitated when a student did not understand the materials they taught, and instead of taking into consideration a different way of explaining the subject, they would holler at the confused student. When I become a teacher I know it is not only my job, but it is my passion to make every student I have understand what I am teaching and enjoy what they are learning. I cannot think of a better reason as to why I want to become a teacher, because I would like to give students a better education then what I experienced.

New Dorp High School was the school I wanted to attend, because it had a Law and History Department that offered students classes more in history and law than in other subjects. I was accepted into that department and couldn't have made my parents and myself more proud. Throughout high school, I maintained the same attitude I had in elementary school, which was to focus only on my studies. This paid off, the principal and many of my teachers noticed my dedication, and I was asked to give speeches to incoming freshman, was captain of the debate team, on the National Honor Society, and was given awards of "Outstanding Excellence," and the "Who's Who Award" annually. Every college I applied to, I received scholarships to.

In my junior year of high school, I was offered an internship in a law firm. Upon my first interview with the attorney, he gave me words of wisdom. The only conversation I had with him changed my mind on becoming a lawyer; he explained the reality of becoming a lawyer, and how much time and dedication you must put into it. He told me that there is no time for a social life until you are about thirty years old. I decided it wasn't a career for me because I wanted to get married and have children before that.

In high school, my life plans were very concrete, and I believed that whatever goal I had was what I would achieve. My dream has always been to raise my children and start a family young. Regardless of all the effort I was putting into my education, I knew that my main goal and priority in life was to be a wife and mother.

CHAPTER 3- A HISTORIAN'S DISCOVERY.

I always had an interest in teaching, but I never focused on making that my career. I wanted to do something in business, because I wanted to make a lot of money. I decided that becoming an accountant was the perfect career for me; it pays well and I could do it from my home when I become a mother. My decision was made in high school, so I applied to every college that offered great business classes. I was accepted to over ten colleges, with scholarships to all. My dream in high school was to go to Pace University, a private university that is well known for its business education. The first year of college, I took business management, accounting, economics, and English classes. I looked forward to my English classes more than I did my business classes. I could not fully understand what the professors taught and the rest of the class was doing better than I was on their tests and essays. After completing a year at Pace University, I decided it was not the school for me. I did not like the commute. More importantly, I did not like the attitude that the professors and students all shared which was very arrogant and made me not feel like I fit in.

I transferred into College of Staten Island. Although the people around me believed that it was a step below Pace, I was very happy. I was able to get a job while going to school full time, because the College is only fifteen minutes from my home. The professors and students were down-to-earth. My first year attending the College of Staten Island, I signed up for all required classes I needed to graduate. CORE 100 is an American History course. In this class, my professor required us to write a paper on what we are interested in, I chose education. In researching for my paper, I realized it was a career I was very captivated by. The art of molding minds and making a difference in children's lives was riveting for me.

In my second term in college I signed up for a class, simply because it fit into my schedule. It was a class that I never knew existed, called "Reacting to the Past," in which the students act out times in history that the professor would assign. Looking back, it was the most fun class I was ever in, and I'm glad I got to be a part of it. I was excited for every class, and I learned so much. The most important lesson I took from this class was that I could teach history. I always enjoyed reading history. And when I analyze myself, I believe that becoming a historian was destined for me. Since I was a child, my family history was the most exciting story that I knew. Throughout elementary and high school, I loved American history. I did great in every class. After school, I would read books by veterans of the Vietnam War and watch the history channel. History was and I believe always will be a true passion of mine.

As I come close to graduation this June, I look back on all the history courses I took, and what I learned. I can graduate from the College of Staten Island with knowledge in world history. My future consists of attending graduate school this September, and trying to find a job as a history teacher. My formal education is my identity, it shaped me to become the person I am today; and it gave me more knowledge then I could have imagined. My story will continue in my experiences of the first hand historical accounts that will be teaching and writing.

And as for CSI and CUNY . . .

As Rosanna comes closer to graduation, she looks back at her CUNY college experience. Her attitude consists of "Could of, would of, should of," rather than "ahh, success!" Like many CUNY students, Rosanna had to overcome many stressful obstacles to get to graduation with a bachelor's degree. One was managing two jobs plus being a full-time student. However, Rosanna feels that even if she wasn't a full time student, she would still be stressed out over one general education class, astronomy, simply because she was uninterested in it. Because it did not grasp her attention, it was difficult to understand what she was being taught, and even more difficult to maintain a high GPA. But Rosanna was aware that this is the general requirement for most, if not all, CUNY colleges, and there was no way of avoiding it.

Rosanna is graduating with a Bachelor's degree and has enough experience to become an excellent teacher, one who will be an inspiration to her students and will leave a lasting impression on them. However, it is almost disgraceful that a BA in History doesn't even come close to making me ready to teach in a classroom, according to CUNY, so Rosanna has only reached a stepping stone. She still must attend Graduate school, take education classes and pass the NYS exams. These days, one degree simply isn't enough to get the career of your dreams. And with Rosanna's passion for history and enthusiasm, she has all the faith in the world that she will one day teach classes with students who will enjoy learning and not just learn to pass the test. Society today doesn't value education, it values a degree; just ask the music and art teachers who are out of work because the city needed to make tax cuts. It proves that we are an uncultured society and prioritize education only that will gain a degree. Rosanna fears that she will one day be in a classroom teaching students who just don't care about the subject and all of her hard work and dedication throughout her CUNY college education will feel like a big waste of time.

Rosanna views the CUNY experience in two ways. Positively, Rosanna is more educated and knows more than her friends and family who didn't go to college; and knowledge is power. Negatively, she had to go through years of stressful classes that were forced on her by CUNY just so that in the long run she can get a job that in reality she has been long been ready for. Another stress from CSI is the disorganization of the school itself. Rosanna graduates in a month, yet she has no idea where and when to get her cap and gown, and where and when the graduation ceremony is. However, Rosanna is a positive person, she always "thinks on the bright side." So she knows that one day, sooner or later, she will say to herself that the nonsense and stress was all worth it.
R.S.

ROSANNA'S CLASSMATES RESPOND

Rosanna has to be the only student in this class who has had an overall positive view of her educational experiences. She has a real concrete hold onto her aspirations in life. Rosanna seems to have negotiated all the differing obstacles of choosing a career, and choose what she had a passion for, teaching. Her father's motivations and commitment to his family curtailed any different career path he might have choose, yet he instilled in his daughter the desire to seek out what you have a passion for and pursue it.

I like how you respected your father and the hardships he went through so you could have a better life. I like it even better that you are doing a lot of this to make him proud and I am sure he will be after it is all said and done. You have a great attitude regarding CUNY which many would say otherwise but since you have both Pace school experience which is a good school and CUNY, I'll take your word for it.

You write, "I transferred into College of Staten Island. Although the people around me believed that it was a step down from Pace, I was very happy." I can most certainly relate to this! It is a shame that the College of Staten Island does not have as high a reputation as other colleges and universities have, but the experience here is quite satisfying. I think you would agree with my viewpoint that one can appreciate a school's experience after transferring from a school where one did not find happiness. I am glad that the change for you was also a healthy one that bolstered your education, and has helped you in making choices about your future career and furthering your education.

I hate when people look down upon the education at CSI. I think we get exactly what we put into it, and for a reasonable price. I have a sister who attends a private college and will be in debt for many years after she graduates, so when people look down on CUNY, I'm perplexed! I assume it's more about the students that attend the school than the actual institution itself. I'm also happy for you, transferring from a school that you weren't content with and moving to CSI seems to have been a positive decision for your life.

Our parents' struggles in their earlier years are something that we share. It seems as though you were very aware of this at such a young age. You recognized this and decided that you wanted to better yourself to avoid being in a similar situation. Sometimes we forget that our parents know best, but I try to heed their advice as much as possible now that I'm a little more mature.

CHAPTER 10:

MARK SESKIN

Second Thoughts

Looking over my essay a second time, I can't but help feel a touch of pride in what I have put to paper as well as what I have achieved as a whole. However there is a lot that I haven't included for the sake of both time and the length of the paper, for example the fact that when I was in preschool a specialist told my mother that I should be institutionalized because I was never going to be normal and she would not be able to handle me as I got older. I kicked him in the shins on the way out and I remember my mom commenting that she wanted to do the same thing! During my middle school years there were a lot of teachers whose names I could have mentioned but didn't. There was also an incident in the school cafeteria when one of the school bullies tried to pick a fight with me and would end up regretting it. He was such a pain that when I hit him back and fought him off, all the kids in the cafeteria and the cafeteria ladies started cheering for me. It made me feel vindicated not just for myself but for all the other kids he picked on constantly.
M.S.

THOMAS JEFFERSON AND ME

In spite of all the recent controversy involving Jefferson and Sally Hemings, the historical image of Thomas Jefferson has always appealed to me. He seemed to be an independent thinker who was above all insistent on keeping our newly formed country from becoming either another royal republic or a social state in which the government is responsible for the welfare of the people. He was looking out for the individual rights of free men to live their lives unfettered by the strings government can frequently impose on its citizens. It has been asserted by some that Jefferson had Asperger's Syndrome and perhaps in part because he was different from others, Jefferson was acutely aware of the fact that the rights of individuals must be preserved by the state.

Thomas Jefferson was born into the land owning gentry class and received an appropriate formal education. In his autobiography, he would later write that his father, Peter Jefferson, "placed me at the English school at 5 years of age and at the Latin at 9, where I continued until his death."[21] Similarly, I have also generally experienced what would be considered to be a normal, middle class education, notwithstanding the differences between then and now.

In his book *Diagnosing Jefferson*, author and historian Norm Ledgin, makes the case that Thomas Jefferson, like myself, had Asperger's Syndrome. His Jefferson study revealed, "A brilliant and talented man who made love to women, tippled his wine, wore funny clothes, abhorred making speeches, fled to seclusion, brooded and wept, sidestepped disputes, waffled on race, obeyed dumb routines, believed fiction real, endured painful losses, and finally went broke."[22]

Like Jefferson, I have also struggled with Asperger's Syndrome. Originally diagnosed as only ADHD, I had a great deal of trouble paying attention and sitting still. Understandably, this caused problems in regular classrooms and many teachers were less than understanding. My real trouble didn't start until first grade. I don't really remember a lot about it, but it was a parochial school and suddenly I was expected to sit in one place for most of the day. My condition was still relatively unknown at the time, and eventually my mother took me out and like Jefferson, I was home

[21] Thomas Jefferson, *Autobiography of Thomas Jefferson*, (New York: Dover Publications, 2005) and "Jefferson's Formal Education," *Thomas Jefferson's Monticello*, Home and Research Collections, http://www.monticello.org/site/research-and-collections/jeffersons-formal-education. (Accessed February, 2012).

[22] Norm Ledgin, "Diagnosing Jefferson" quoted in Lawrence Osborne's, *American Normal: The Hidden World of Asperger Syndrome* (New York: Copernicus Books, 2002), Kindle Edition, Location 1905.

schooled. I did very well at home following my own pace, and at the end of a year I was able to read and write on a third grade level. Unfortunately I cannot compare this to Jefferson since very little is known about Jefferson's childhood. Jefferson's childhood home was burnt to the ground destroying records, and his parents died while he was still a fairly young man.

However we know that the gentry of Virginia followed the English model which emphasized appropriate education, not a degree. Jefferson's later studies at William and Mary College followed a course which was appropriate for English gentlemen. Rather than a degree, which would have led to a career in the Anglican Church or as a college professor, his seven years of study allowed him to practice law without any type of degree.[23] My parents too, were more concerned that I receive a good, solid, education than a degree. They sent me to a Montessori School for second through fifth grades. It was overall an enjoyable experience because I was allowed and even encouraged to do my work at my own pace and explore my interests. Moreover I could sit anywhere I wanted. There were carpet mats which we were expected to use to sit on the floor and there were even places where we could lie down and work. My biggest difficulty here was in socialization. I was quiet and tended to keep to myself. It was during this time that I began to take karate classes both for self-defense and to help improve focus and concentration. It wasn't a cure but it helped considerably.

> Later in life, Jefferson expressed an analogous opinion that the standard course of study which led to a degree was not the wisest use of time and suggested that students concentrate on a course of study which would ultimately be useful to them. He said,

This relinquishes the honorary distinction of a Diploma, a good enough thing to excite the ambition of youth to study, but, in modern estimation,

[23] "Jefferson's Formal Education," online transcript of a Telephone interview with Stacy Gould, Archivist of Special Collections, Swem Library at the College of William and Mary, 1999. http://www.monticello.org/site/research-and-collections/jeffersons-formal-education. (Accessed February, 2012).

no longer worth tacking its initials to one's name; and certainly not worth the sacrifice of a single useful science.[24]

Unfortunately, Montessori school ended with fifth grade after which I had to attend a public middle school where again I was expected to sit for long periods of time and take notes. At this point in time I was diagnosed with Asperger's Syndrome and like Jefferson, I too was introverted, had difficulty connecting with people, and was sensitive to criticism and noise.[25]

Here again on the previous problems, socialization was my worst enemy. I was the kid who was always picked on. To make matters worse, the teachers at IS2 didn't seem to care and refused to intervene when any of the students were being bullied. Their basic attitude was that I was making up problems or just looking for attention. Justifiably, I was frustrated and extremely irritated by this. To add to my problems, many of the teachers and even the school administration were resistant to any suggestions my parents made on my behalf. Basically they saw me as a troubled child who should be shipped off to special education because they believed I wasn't intelligent enough to deal with the curriculum. Eventually, after a great deal of negotiation between the principal and my parents, I was given a one-on-one paraprofessional. Things finally started to improve and I made it to the honor rolls and graduated.

I went on to New Dorp High School, and for all its faults, it wasn't remotely as bad as Egbert Middle School. They were better set up to deal with kids like me and I had a wonderful para who stayed with me for the entire four years of high school. She didn't just treat me as a student; she treated me like I was her own son, and I attribute much of my success to her. The teachers were far more understanding and as always I had the support of my parents.

---

[24] "Jefferson's Formal Education," Jefferson to Eppes, 16 September 1821.University of Virginia. http://www.monticello.org/site/research-and-collections/jeffersons-formal-education. (Accessed February, 2012).

[25] Jonathan Mitchell, "Undiagnosing Gates, Jefferson and Einstein," http://www.jonathans-stories.com/non-fiction/undiagnosing.html#Thomas Jefferson http://www.jonathans-stories.com/non-fiction/undiagnosing.html#Thomas Jefferson. (Accessed February, 2012).

25

Here again, like Jefferson, I was able to benefit from a personalized educational experience. It was during high school that my writing style developed into what it is today. I was in the College Now Program and we were drilled to read, write, and comprehend on a college level from our freshman year. We were taught to use MLA format and our spelling, grammar, and attention to sources had to be up to standards.

College has had its own rough spots but far less than middle school or high school. Although I didn't have a para anymore, I learned to take notes for myself. I get a great deal of help from the good people at the disabilities office, who help me deal with any problems I encounter. Through the disabilities office I have made friends and acquaintances, who like me, have some degree of disability to deal with. All in all college has been a positive experience. However I understand that this is not the end of my education but actually a jumping off point.

Jefferson had three honorary degrees and justifiably could have used them after his name if had chosen to, but he did not.[26] Instead, Jefferson used his knowledge, particularly the classic languages of Latin and Greek, to extend his self-education in a wide array of subjects. This can be confirmed by a letter he wrote to Joseph Priestly in January of 1800 where he stated:

> I thank on my knees, who directed my early education, for having put into my possession this rich source of delight [knowledge of Greek and Latin]; and I would not exchange it for anything which I could then have acquired, and have not since acquired.[27]

In other words Jefferson, like Henry Adams, felt that real education comes from life experiences and seeking out things that interest one. Even at an early age, I was fascinated with geology, rocks and bones, as well as dinosaurs and other extinct animals, which seemed to capture my

26 "Jefferson's Formal Education," Jefferson to Joseph Priestly, 1800 January 27. Primary Source Reference, University of Virginia. http://www.monticello.org/site/research-and-collections/jeffersons-formal-education. (accessed February, 2012)

* "Jefferson's Formal Education," from an article based on Gaye Wilson, Monticello Research Report, December 1999. http://www.monticello.org/site/research-and-collections/jeffersons-formal-education. (Accessed February, 2012).

imagination. Although Jefferson had a wide array of interests, one which we have in common is our enthusiasm for geology and paleontology. In 1797, Thomas Jefferson published a paper about his discovery of a new species and it was consequently named after him. Jefferson demonstrated a common Asperger's syndrome trait of obsessing on a particular area. In this case it was his fascination with finding large prehistoric creatures in the American wilderness. His discovery was a huge claw which he recovered from a cave in West Virginia. Initially Jefferson believed that his find belonged to a sort of lion, which would have been three times larger than those in Africa and named it Megalonyx.[28]

It later turned out to be a giant ground sloth. However, it was nonetheless a new species, and it was eventually named, jeffersoni after the now president, Jefferson.[29] Jefferson's Ground Sloth, Megalonyx jeffersoni lived in the area, which is now Virginia, during the Ice Age and became extinct around 9,000 years ago. Today their closest living relatives are the much smaller tree sloths, armadillos, and anteaters. They may have looked somewhat like bears and were huge and bulky, but like their present day counterparts, were slow-moving herbivores, eating lcavcs and twigs of woody plants. They were about 20 feet long and weighed roughly 3 to 4 tons. Today a model giant ground sloth, named Clawd, is on display at the Virginia Museum of Natural History.[30]

Because of his work, Jefferson is recognized for his early contributions to the science of vertebrate paleontology in North America. Jefferson also sponsored important work on mastodons, when he later became president of the American Philosophical Society in Philadelphia.[31]

Moreover, Jefferson's *Notes on the State of Virginia* catalogs and examines topography, soils, climate, minerals, plants and animals, as well as stream flows, lakes and coastlines. Jefferson's geological contributions helped

[28] Richard Coniff, "The President Discovers a Species," The Species Seekers: Heroes, Fools and the Mad Pursuit of Life on Earth. , http://strangebehaviors.wordpress.com/2011/02/09/the-president-discovers-a-species/ Feb 9, 2001. (Accessed Feb, 2011).
29 Coniff.
[30] Jefferson's Ground Sloth, "Clawd," Virginia Museum of Natural History. http://www.vmnh.net/index.cfm/topic/clawd.
[31] Coniff,

paved the way for later geologists. A century later, the U.S. Geological Survey used the section involving rivers as a prototype. His analysis of minerals is also used as a pattern for mineral surveys still published by the U.S. Geological Survey. In his *Notes*, Jefferson, on his own, also developed the idea that time lines could be drawn according to layers of soil. Today this is referred to as superpositioning, which states that if there is no disturbance of soil layers, that the youngest layer of rocks and fossils must be at the top and gets older with each successive layer.[32]

In the Paris edition of *Notes* (1785), Jefferson discussed his chemical theory of the formation of shells found on mountaintops. It "brought [Jefferson] considerable criticism because it was inconsistent with the Biblical account of Noah's flood."[33] Jefferson wrote and perfected *Notes* when he was in his late thirties, before his involvement in politics. Historians are in general agreement that Jefferson was thin-skinned about criticism and became more so with age,[34] conceivably another symptom of Asperger's Syndrome. In 1803, Jefferson wrote:

> Every word which goes from me, whether verbally or in writing becomes the subject of so much malignant distortion, and perverted construction, that I am obliged to caution my friends against…my letters getting into the public.[35]

Like Jefferson I too have had a lifelong obsession with geology and paleontology. In fact my minor is in Geology and I hope to take more courses at another university which offers Geology as a major. It is my hope to one day go on a paleontological dig as part of this and, like Jefferson, I too have always yearned to find a new species and have it named after me. In many ways History and Geology are subjects which are parallel to one another. I believe that each offers an insight into the events of the past. My knowledge of geology has often aided in analyzing historical problems,

32 "Geology," Thomas Jefferson's Monticello, Home and Research Collections, http://www.monticello.org/site/research-and-collections/geology. (Accessed February, 2012).

33 Ibid.

34 Ibid.

35 Jefferson to Edward Dowse, Washington, April 19, 1803, "Geology," Thomas Jefferson's Monticello, Home and Research Collections, http://www.monticello.org/site/research-and-collections/geology. (Accessed February, 2012).

particularly in ancient history. Moreover, learning to use the scientific method has enabled me to stand back and analyze historical situations more dispassionately.

As far as my religious values are concerned, like Jefferson, I tend toward deism. Jefferson was generally reluctant to reveal his personal religious beliefs. Raised as an Anglican, he was influenced by English deists, particularly Bolingbroke and Shaftesbury.[36] A great deal of his religious philosophy is revealed in a comment he made to his nephew Peter Carr in 1787, "Question with boldness even the existence of a god; because, if there be one, he must more approve the homage of reason, than that of blindfolded fear."[37] Here we can see the influence of Enlightenment thinking on Jefferson in regard to religious ideology.

In Query XVII of his *Notes on the State of Virginia*, however, he plainly states his ideas regarding the separation of church and state:

> The rights of conscience we never submitted, we could not submit. We are answerable for them to our God. The legitimate powers of government extend to such acts only as are injurious to others. But it does me no injury for my neighbour to say there are twenty gods, or no god. It neither picks my pocket nor breaks my leg. ... Reason and free enquiry are the only effectual agents against error. [38]

These ideas ultimately led to the passage of the *Statute of Virginia for Religious Freedom*. Jefferson's religious views became a major public issue during the bitter party conflict between Federalists and Republicans in the late 1790s, when Jefferson was often accused of being an atheist.

---

[36] "Jefferson's Religious Beliefs," Thomas Jefferson's Monticello, Home and Research Collections, Thomas Jefferson Encyclopedia, http://www.monticello.org/site/research-and-collections/jeffersons-religious-beliefs. (Accessed February, 2012).

[37] Thomas Jefferson to Peter Carr, 10 August 1787, "Jefferson's Religious Beliefs," Thomas Jefferson's Monticello, Home and Research Collections, Thomas Jefferson Encyclopedia, http://www.monticello.org/site/research-and-collections/jeffersons-religious-beliefs. (Accessed February, 2012).

[38] "Jefferson's Religious Beliefs", from Notes on the State of Virginia, edited by William Peden, (Chapel Hill: University of North Carolina Press, 1955) 159. http://www.monticello.org/site/research-and-collections/jeffersons-religious-beliefs. (Accessed February, 2012).

In comparison, I am not a highly religious individual. I believe that there is a God and a heaven and a hell, but much like Henry Adams, I'm not one for organized religion. There have been so many wars promulgated by organized religions. Each believes that theirs is the only way to worship the supreme deity. Also, because of my condition, I am both unwilling and unable to sit and listen to someone lecture me about morality, which I believe to be strictly a personal matter. I am the product of a Christian mother and a Jewish father. While we celebrate the big holidays like Christmas and Passover, it is generally a secular affair, involving family, friends and a great deal of food. I am also in complete agreement with Jefferson that Church and State must remain separate. I don't believe the church has any business running our government and I don't think the government has any business being involved in religion. I am also a political conservative and like Jefferson, I don't want big government interfering in things I believe are personal matters, whether religious or financial.

I must admit that a large part of my fascination with Jefferson is the fact that he had some kind of personality disorder. This was not the Jefferson we read about in our history books, but a man with quirks and problems who managed in spite of everything, to live a full and successful life. He is certainly a role model for those of us who are not average and never will be.

Perhaps the most workable definition of Asperger's Syndrome comes from researchers and writers at the Yale Child Study Center:

Lack of empathy; naive, inappropriate, one-sided social interaction, little ability to form friendships and consequent social isolation; pedantic and monotonic speech; intense absorption in circumscribed topics conveying the impression of eccentricity; and in some cases clumsy and ill-coordinated movements and odd posture.[39]

For those of us with Asperger's, the most obvious cognitive disability is social. In essence, for reasons that are not yet understood, people with Asperger's cannot read the human face or its emotions. This is an ability normal people seem to be born with.

---

[39] Osborne, *American Normal*, Location 40.

> Aspies, as we call ourselves, have great difficulty learning social rules and fine distinctions. Although frequently talented intellectually, we have to be taught to recognize the simplest social cue or hint.[40]

As far as Asperger's traits, Jefferson seems to have had several, including impairment in his use of nonverbal behaviors like eye-to-eye contact, facial expressions, and body postures. He also exhibited some inflexibility in his routines and was observed to have some rituals. Although some have commented on his lack of social or emotional reciprocity, he was apparently comfortable enough with those he knew to be relaxed and jovial. Like Jefferson, I don't like speaking in public and frequently stutter. I tend to become nervous in big crowds and feel uncomfortable with making eye to eye contact. When I'm stressed, I also tend to do specific rituals like murmur to myself and pace.

According to many eyewitnesses, Jefferson's quirks were numerous enough to justify a psychiatric suggestion of Asperger's Syndrome. For one thing, he began each day by soaking his feet in icy water. Among his other Asperger-like symptoms are that he paced back and forth or in circles when upset, he often spoke in a strange monotone voice, he was a loner, he would often neglect his grooming needs, and seemed to be hypersensitive to some sounds while being simultaneously super-tolerant toward others. He was said to have 'sang under his breath constantly,' and it was often observed that he displayed a stiff posture, and had an inexpressive facial expression. Most importantly, he seemed unable to sense the feelings of others. All of the above have been cited as proof that Jefferson had Asperger's Syndrome.[41] Although I am not always aware of it, I tend to do many of these things myself. I am inclined to speak or hum under my breath, and twitch, *etc.* Also like Jefferson there are some sounds I just can't tolerate while I'm completely fine with others. Moreover I am not always aware of it when I'm speaking in a volume that some consider overly loud. Sometimes people

---

[40] Osborne, *American Normal*, Location 45.

[41] Osborne, *American Normal*, Location 45.

think I am shouting at them and I am unaware of the fact that my volume is causing distress in others.

Another symptom of Asperger's was Jefferson's refusal to wear abrasive fabrics of any kind. He liked soft, flexible materials. This has always been a problem for me. I'm not sure why, but abrasive fabrics generally make me more hyper and twitchy than when I am wearing cottons or other soft fabrics. To me it feels like having needles scratching my skin.

According to Ledgin, perhaps Jefferson's most significant Asperger's symptom was his lifelong obsession with his unfinished mansion at Monticello, which according to Ledgin, meets the criterion of an encompassing, abnormal, preoccupation. Even Jefferson seems to confirm some of these ideas when he said, "The whole of my life has been a war with my natural tastes, feelings and wishes."[42]

Jefferson died at the age of eighty three in 1826 on the 50th anniversary of the adoption of the Declaration of Independence. He accomplished a prodigious amount of work, in widely diverse fields, in spite of his handicaps. Jefferson's last wish was that his gravestone proclaim the positive things he had accomplished in his lifetime. These were obviously the things of which he was most proud. His epitaph reads:

> HERE WAS BURIED THOMAS JEFFERSON AUTHOR OF THE DECLARATION OF AMERICAN INDEPENDENCE OF THE STATUTE OF VIRGINIA FOR RELIGIOUS LIBERTY AND FATHER OF THE UNIVERSITY OF VIRGINIA[43]

As for CSI and CUNY . .

This assignment was also a challenge because I was basically asked to write my memoirs and compare myself with a man who lived until his late eighties and died about one hundred and fifty years before even my grandparents were

[42] Osborne, *American Normal*, Location 1730.

[43] "A Brief Biography of Thomas Jefferson," Thomas Jefferson's Monticello, Home and Research Collections, http://www.monticello.org/site/jefferson/brief-biography-thomas-jefferson. (Accessed February, 2012).

born. It also didn't help that a large portion of the records about Jefferson's early years were lost in a fire. Still I think I did a fairly good job comparing myself and Jefferson as well as finding out that I had a bit more in common with one of the founding fathers than I had originally assumed. I hope this helps others kids and young adults in a similar position as me. Just because you have a disability, such as Asperger's Syndrome, doesn't mean you are restricted in what you can do. It is also kind of ironic that the campus of CSI is built on the site of the former Willowbrook Institution so that in a very strange way, I was institutionalized after all!
M.S.

MARK'S CLASSMATES RESPOND

I have to commend Mark on a very comprehensive review of his life. For someone in his early 20s he seems to have developed an understanding of the world in which people are not all the same and that we all have not only different personalities, but different and special life stories. When I was his age, I assumed all of humanity was the same in terms of behavior, except of course for a few sad cases of crazy people. Other than that, everyone seemed to be the same in terms of norms of behavior.

In spite of having Asperger's Syndrome with slight behavioral tics, you seem normal to me. By the way Mark, we all have our behavioral idiosyncrasies, even if they are not readily apparent to the untrained eye.

I am glad that like Jefferson, you too believe in separation of church and state. You say that being a political conservative, "like Jefferson, I don't want big government interfering in things I believe are personal matters, whether religious or financial." I must inform you Mark, that politically conservative "Red" states have passed laws which for all practical purposes, have banned or restricted contraception for women, doing everything they can to control a woman's body. Also, financial regulations are needed to prevent greedy businessmen from stealing people's money with Ponzi-schemed practices.

—

Mark gives me a chance to see first-hand that my contemporaries in history have limitless talents in which I can benefit immensely, by allowing myself to learn from them. The comparisons by Mark to Jefferson, taught me more about Jefferson than anyone else in a history class. I am sure I will be using Mark's paper as a reference tool of citation in future papers. Mark gave me an education in the struggles, but more to the point, the successes of a student with Asperger's.

—

Mark I thought you had one of the best papers I've read in of the class. You are an extremely bright guy and I applaud you and the hardships you had to endure growing up. People can be cruel but I like your attitude on how you used it to your advantage. I'm not too sure about Jefferson and the condition(s) he had but all I know is if you run for president you got my vote.

—

Being bullied can be one of the most traumatizing things for a young student. It seems like you not only overcame this, but you were able to persevere. Everyone's past shaped them for the future, and you are one of the brightest kids in class. Your paper only reinforces this.

Mark, I commend you for comparing yourself to a historical figure in your paper in order to discuss your education.

When reading Mark Seskin's educational story I was beginning to form many thoughts. My first thought was I had two classes with Mark and I believe he is highly intellectual. Mark compares himself with Thomas Jefferson who may have had Asperger's Syndrome. Thomas Jefferson is one of the founding fathers. I would have to say Jefferson was limitless in his own era. He was not diagnosed or given this label. Labels such as Asperger's Syndrome, ADD/ADHD or autism were not given till later on. He was also able to write out or voice out his own opinions. He was able to socialize. I believe labels make individuals feel they are not normal. If Jefferson did have Asperger Syndrome I would tell all those who have been diagnosed with this syndrome to ignore the label and just be who you are. The reason why I would say this is because Jefferson if he had Asperger's Syndrome did not have to deal with this label. He was not told that he was different. This gives evidence that if Jefferson did have Asperger's Syndrome he was able to teach himself how to function and cope with the symptoms of Asperger's Syndrome on his own. They tell individuals with Asperger Syndrome they have poor social skills but in the case of Jefferson he taught himself how to socialize. Jefferson had a best friend that he grew up with. Mark, we live in an era where anything that does not fit the word normal or the narrow approach in the educational system is instantly labeled. You just learn differently and this to me means you have learning abilities. If everyone learned the same the world would be a boring place. If everyone learned the same and had the same strategies cures would not develop. Technologies would not appear. Comic books would not be created. There is a purpose for every individual. If every general in war had the same strategies every battle would be lost. The human abilities are all different and the terminology of normal needs to change. If you really analyze Jefferson's life of possibly having Asperger Syndrome you maybe the very person who finds the coping method, the teaching method, the very solution of Asperger Syndrome.

Mark has had to endure the terrible situation of being bullied as a kid. My wish, after being inspired by his paper, is for the future parents of America to realize the harm that bullying can do. I also wish that Mark realizes how impressive and well written his paper is.

CHAPTER 11:
PATRICK SLYMAN

I never thought I would ever put the education system on trial as I do in the following pages. My intention was to write an autobiographical essay and hope to learn about myself in the process. I achieved my original goal and so much more. My education has been a life-long process up to this point, and is still in its early stages. Furthermore, through my scrutiny of the education system, and my thanks for it, I feel it is my duty to make a career out of being a part of it, and improving it.

My feelings about the educational institutions that I have been a part of have never been so apparent to me until I began writing this autobiography. I, like many other students, was told I had to get an education, and considered school to be a part of life, something one must accept. Unbeknownst to me, I was actually accruing opinions on each step of my education and comparing them to the steps I had experienced before. While learning school subjects, I was also learning how to learn, and through comparison, developing negative feelings about the systems of learning that had failed me.

This essay is not meant to be an attack or praise to any one institution in the field of education or in life; it is meant to be a summary of my life, my experiences, and my feelings towards the obstacles I have been presented with. Whether deemed positive or negative, every milestone in my life has been met with the utmost open-mindedness, and it has only been through comparison of something newer and better that I have concluded that something previously given to me had a negative impact. Much like this paper itself, each new educational experience opens my eyes to the fact that no matter how much you know, there is so much knowledge in this world that you will never even begin

to grasp. With that in mind, I give you the following analysis of my own life through the eyes of a young, unfinished student.
P.S.

Patrick Slyman, that being the name they gave to him, finds it hypocritical to say he has had an education, whether a good one or not, to describe. This is primarily due to the fact that he realizes if one can say that he or she is truly educated, it blinds him to the fact that it may actually be the contrary. If one has been through life yet never had the fortune of being given an authentic education, he can still call his life experiences and first-hand accounts his own education. Yet Patrick understands that only the truly educated can compare his own education to that of those around him. These are the details of his life, making up his unfinished education.

Since he was in utero, Patrick was very much an independent, sending his mother into labor three months early. He was ready to take this world on for all it was willing to give. On the twenty-seventh day of March in the year A.D 1990, while George Herbert Walker Bush was presiding over the United States during the peaceful end of the Cold War, a healthy young Patrick was born to Tammy and Thomas Slyman, their second of what would be a total of three children. While the world around him was full of uncertainty, Patrick was one who would be sure of his role in whatever situation he found himself.

Patrick's childhood in Staten Island was a jovial one. He was a fast learner, was interested in activities and games, and was thrilled to have frequent visits by his family, including his mother's parents, whom he adored. Patrick's grandmother and grandfather played a crucial role in the earliest stages of his education. Teaching him wisdom at a young age, they taught him the basic necessities to prepare him for the world he was so ready to embrace. The quest for an education began at an early age for Patrick. Reading, writing, and music were interests of his long before his formal education would begin. Patrick began playing piano at a young age, with very limited success. However, his experiences early on with music and its rudiments would stick with Patrick forever.

One of the earliest experiences that he can remember, now being a twenty-one year old man, is the first sign of significant pain Patrick faced. He was no older then thirty-six months of age, and it was a bright and glorious day. Running around and playing with his older brother as he so often did, Patrick slipped and fell, sliding head first into the corner of the refrigerator door. The end result of this first catastrophe in Patrick's life was seven stitches, a semi-major loss of blood, and a valuable lesson learned. Before this event, he had not yet learned the anatomy and physiology of the human being. Raised Catholic up to this point, he knew little about Earth and the humans that inhabit it. As far back as he could remember, of which signs are still obvious today, Patrick had the assumption that he was indestructible, that no matter what he did, he could not be harmed, that he was more than a biological human, but was instead something greater. Throughout his life, any sign of caution in any situation can be traced back to this event, for it was then he realized that he was mortal. Physically, emotionally, and mentally, this event changed young Patrick's view on life, and the way he embraced it. For his age, Patrick was still somewhat reckless, but was also conscious of the effects of his actions as well. These traits he took with him to his first form of formal education: kindergarten class at St. Ann's School, in his hometown of Staten Island.

Coming from a small family, which at this point consists of two married parents, and two children close in age, Patrick was used to being sheltered. His father worked for the City of New York as a correction officer, while his mother quit her job at the World Trade Center to stay home and raise her two young boys. He was a happy young boy, the baby of the family, always being taken care of by his older brother and parents. Entering his formal education, Patrick had already learned so much, and at five years old, wanted only to learn more and more. The next ten years of his life would play a large role on what he learned, as well as his ability to learn it.

St. Ann's School is a formal school that educates Catholic children in all subjects from kindergarten to eighth grade. For Patrick, this lasted nine years, from 1995-2004, when he graduated with honors. His first teacher, a nun, was probably the strictest. This was ironic for Patrick because it made the years following kindergarten to be quite easy. For Patrick, having a strict teacher early on was of no benefit, for it was in his later years of formal learning that he needed an extra push, a push he didn't get until graduating from grammar school. Year by year, he graduated with straight As. Unfortunately, grammar school was not a challenge for young Patrick. Quite the contrary, Catholic grammar school was a nuisance to his education. For the time he spent at school and on schoolwork during those years, Patrick always felt he did not get enough in return. Rather, he was pushed through grade by grade, doing what the teachers asked with little actual effort. For hours a day he would sit in class reading, writing, and observing. This had a great effect on his education, but not in the way the institution intended.

Patrick was always more of an observational, hands-on learner than a learner by means of studying. Not to say Patrick did not enjoy reading, for he so loved it; but on the topic of learning, he did a better job in the field, as he will come to find out later on. Before Patrick could see what he wanted from the world around him, he had to work with what he was given, and during these years, he was given a biased education by the Catholic institution. This was also used in his advantage, for it opened his eye to the world of religion and its inner and outer workings. Patrick was not one to break rules, so he did as he was told in school and at home. Unfortunately for him, this consisted of reading and writing about religion, and attending masses and participating in prayer. None of this came off as being out of the ordinary for young Patrick. He saw everyone else participating just as he was. Therefore, he accepted it as the norm, and did not question the system. By the time Patrick had gotten to eighth grade and was thirteen years of age, he began to ask questions. For he knew that he was approaching the end of his formal Catholic education. In embracing this fact, he had many questions about the real world that he had heard so much about, and was about to become familiar with, questions that would be answered through the experiences that awaited him.

Patrick's life in St Ann's was not a negative one. He met great people, made many friends and memories that he still carries with him today, and took advantage of the fact that getting a Catholic education and a public education gave him the opportunity to compare opposite sides of the education system, and choose what he believed to be the better one and pursue what it had to offer. Luckily for Patrick, he knew this at a moderately young age. By the middle of eighth grade he knew that there was no turning back, that he had to choose whether or not he would further his education as a Catholic, or he would make a blind attempt in searching for something more, something that there was no guarantee would be there. Although he was thankful for the little education that the Catholic institution had given him, Patrick knew at that time that he wanted something more, something he would not get if he allowed himself to be babied through school, having his hand held while at the same time being forced to worship a phony god and a phony book written by a bunch of mere men.

By eighth grade Patrick began to question his religion. He was full of questions and was aware of the biases that the religion forced on him brought with it. He knew the answers to his questions, questions that would further his pursuit of education the way he wanted it could only be answered if he chose to take on sources outside of those that had been made available to him thus far. At fourteen, Patrick renounced his ties to the Catholic religion and began a high school education funded by the city of New York.

Almost immediately, Patrick saw the vast change in the way things were run in the public school system. Coming from a class of thirty-five students, and one teacher per grade, Patrick was now presented with seven different teachers per semester, and a freshman class size of almost one thousand. This was just another detail which Patrick welcomed with the utmost optimism. For the first time, he was fully responsible for himself. He would not have his hand held and have his future and education decided for him. His life, his education, his future, for the first time, were all in his hands, and at the ripe age of fourteen years old, Patrick took full advantage of this fact.

Things had become more and more clear in his studies throughout high school, especially in history and science. Suddenly, gaps in North American as well as world history, left vacant in Catholic funded textbooks, had been filled, and not with nonsense, but with facts backed by evidence. Suddenly, a new world had opened up for Patrick. His previous education became void. Through the next four years he would read more than he had read in his life prior. It was almost as if he wanted to start his education over from the very beginning. He began to embrace his formal education, and savor every minute of it. He now understood the value of what he was being taught, and took advantage. It was during this time that the historian was born.

A lot had begun to happen very rapidly for Patrick. He was in a new school with a new outlook on his own life and education. He began to analyze his life, what it had become and what it was before. The transition from Catholic school to public school was an immense one. He knew the possibilities were endless. All he once knew and believed was now gone, and in its place was hope, wonder, and a world of information and education waiting for him.

What he appreciated most at this point were his studies in history, the way things actually happened. He would sit in class with his full attention given to the teacher, eating up the information that was given to him. He had such a love for history that all the books and lectures in the world could not fill. As he began to pay more and more attention to his teachers, something else happened. Along with the histories that had seemed to change with the school setting, so did the pedagogy involved in them. After the initial excitement began to settle down, Patrick was like any other student, simply enjoying his education. What came next for him in all his classes, but more so in history, was his understanding and observation of the teachers. Patrick knew just as much as many of his teachers.

The next challenge for him was to present what he knew the way they did. He was never that good as a speaker. He was a much better writer. Yet, something drew him to the art of presentation, of lecturing, of passing information and doing it in an effective manner. Pretty soon, another change had begun to happen for the boy. In his studies of history and pedagogy, he had begun to adore a number of his teachers. He had great respect for most of them and the work that they did, as well as the impact they had on him as a student. However, there were a number of teachers that were wasting his time, not giving him the education he was in search of. The combination of seeing two opposite professors within forty-five minutes of one another, as well as his newfound love for history, is what instilled in the young fragile mind of Patrick that it was his destiny to be a teacher. For he so loved this world, and its history, and he so loved and valued education, for he was living proof that education, when used in its most effective manner, can change the lives of students. It seemed like destiny, although the young boy did not believe in such a thing, this was the closest to any sign of it that he had seen to date.

Only a couple of years into becoming an independent thinker Patrick found what it was he wanted to do. It was this dream that he had begun to chase, a little at a time, and he never gave up. Throughout his high school years, through friends, family, and time, he never gave up on this dream. Never before had he been so motivated to learn. In nine years of Catholic school the only thing education seemed to him was a nuisance. This was not, however, because he was by any means a bad or lazy student, it was because the system he was given did not work for him. Patrick, in order to reach his fullest potential, needed independence. He needed the free will to go out and find what worked for him, and that's exactly what he did.

Eight years later, he is still chasing the same dream. Although someone like Henry Adams would disagree with any formal education, perhaps he would agree with the idea that education is in the hands of the student, and he or she must go find whatever it is they hope to achieve. This turned out to be true for Patrick because what he was looking for was presented in the form of formal education. History and pedagogy can be found elsewhere, but the best way to compare them and use them together would be found in formal education institutions. Furthermore, the fact that he was given the opportunity to have gone to both Catholic and public schools, therefore being able to compare the two, contributed just as much to his wanting to become a teacher as his love for history and pedagogy.

Well into college, Patrick's love for history, reading, and education only grew with time. He was still following his dream to become a history teacher. Having seen the pros and cons of both Catholic and public school, he wisely chose to continue his education at a nearby public institution, the College of Staten Island. Patrick, now eighteen years of age, chose to continue with what worked best for him up to this point. Also, he felt it his duty to continue in the public education field, hoping he could one day return to that field and inspire students just as he himself was inspired.

As his education continued, Patrick began to want to learn more. He began taking more elective classes, trying to round out his education, but always return to history and pedagogy. He adored pedagogy so much because it was the art of learning that he loved more than anything, and wanted to pass on. To become a teacher, and further his own education, well contributing to that of others would be nothing short of a dream come true for young Patrick. His consistency in the field shows his dedication, as his education is not yet complete, and may never be.

Through his years in college, Patrick took up a part time job in the emergency room of Staten Island University Hospital as a nursing assistant. Work ethic has been another part of Patrick's education that he has never given up. Having been working since he was thirteen years old when he had his own paper route, he has continually held a job until the present date. His only reason for leaving one job was because a better opportunity had presented itself. Just as in his education, he was open to try newer, more beneficial experiences in the work field. His jobs ranged from a paper route, to various retail stores, a five-year tenure as an assistant carpenter, to his current three-year tenure as a nursing assistant. His job experience is fairly broad, just like his educational experiences. His formal education experiences taught him that there is always something bigger and better out there, and it is up to the individual to get it for himself or herself.

Throughout his life we have seen him do just that, both in his education, and in his work experiences.

As an historian, Patrick's study is one that will forever be unfinished, for no one man in this world can say he or she knows everything that history has to offer. This does not mean that Patrick would not call his education a rewarding one. Since the events unfolded leading him to make the decision to go into the field of history, Patrick has valued his education. He works hard each day to ensure that it only grows. For one person to dedicate that much time and interest into one specific subject without being forced to do so, it is safe to say that he has an admiration for the field. It has been that admiration that has driven Patrick to never give up until his goals are reached, and even beyond that. His drive to learn is one that seems to never slow down. Although he is in the early stages of his education, as well as in his life, the love of learning and the attitude towards striving to get the best education is what keeps the undergraduate learning, and searching for new ways to do so. While the boy is satisfied with his education as an historian and as an educator, he understands that his own education is one from which he will never graduate. He incorporates his life experiences into his education. Therefore, he never stops learning. Seeing the flaws in his early education has taught him to filter his future education, ensuring he will learn only what promises to help him reach his goal as a truly educated man, educated in the same sense as Henry Adams.

As for CSI and CUNY . . .

Analyzing my education is what brought me to the step in my education that I am currently at. As a product of the Catholic and public education system, there is one major factor in my own education that I have not provided my judgment to just yet, simply because I have not had the full experience of it yet, of course I am talking about the City University of New York system, more specifically, College of Staten Island.

I was introduced the CUNY world in the summer of 2008. Coming off the best four years in my education, I was full of hope and wonder for what lied ahead (unlike four years prior, when my Catholic school education had me full of pessimism and regret). Although the College of Staten Island was my only option due to financial and residential restrictions, my mind was still ripe, and ready to be filled with whatever wonderful information was in store at CSI.

Almost immediately in my CSI career was I given the impression of the institution that still resides with me today, four years later. Coming from St. Ann's, I was not fully prepared for public high school. This was because I was so used to a biased, small-classroom, childish approach to education. Entering New Dorp High School was almost the opposite. I was given more teachers, more points-of-view, more resources, more books, and most importantly, the ability to get an education on the level that I chose for myself. Electives, level of challenge, and extracurricular activities were now my choice, rather than a path already being laid out for me. The transition from New Dorp High School to CSI proved to be just as surprising as the last, and was even more of a shock to me. Coming from public High School ready to embark on four years of community college led me to believe that I knew what I was getting into, that it would be just like before. I was wrong.

CSI was even more abundant than New Dorp. A larger library, more computers, more faculty, CSI proved to be bigger and more plentiful than New Dorp. This excited me, and I was ready to embrace it. This is when I experienced the major difference between my high school and college. While New Dorp's administrators are almost entirely made up of former teachers, CSI's directors are mostly bureaucrats that may know how to run a business, but have no idea how to run an institution.

This minor difference in these two public schools led to a world of troubles for me over the next four years. While the resources at CSI may have been exceptional, accessing them is just the opposite. Everything from student parking, to registering for classes, to graduating on time seems to be purposely made difficult for the student. This causes students to lose interest and resent something that they should be embracing. The level of education at CSI is exceptional because it is built on the backs of hard working, underpaid, Ph.D. certified employees. Anyone who wants to learn is bound to get an exceptional education through the school. But after Catholic school tried to force a biased education into my fragile young mind, and public high school allowed me to build my own education, CSI seemed to work against me. And from what I understand about the entire CUNY system, the other schools involved in it do just the same.

I would never take back anything I learned at CSI. I was given exceptional knowledge from exceptional people in my four years spent at the institution. However, I have learned that while a good education needs to be earned by the individual, it should never, under any circumstances, be made unavailable.
P.S.

PATRICK'S CLASSMATES RESPOND

I too had gone to both public and private schools. I can honestly say that private schools to me are a just a cheap way of taking money from their students and parents. I feel like I learned more in public schools than private. If a student has the ability, drive and termination to want an education, just about any school will do without having to put a price tag on it.

I am also one who has attended both Catholic and public schools. My education in these schools differed greatly. In public school, I felt like math was stressed more. In Catholic school, it was more about grammar and English. It was also supposed to be a college prep school, but the only time we did SAT work was the week leading up to the exam.

In the classroom Patrick was always angry at the Catholic Church concerning being inculcated with religious dogma in which he says "He was given a biased education by the Catholic institution" of elementary parochial school. His disillusionment he annunciated in the classroom had spread to a formal rejection of the faith in which he was raised. Professor Powers tried to gently nudge him into thinking of something about the Catholic faith that had some ameliorating qualities.

In Patrick's life essay, however, the volatile fire and brimstone of denunciation is missing. Everything is formally announced in a well-thought-out derivation as if it were instructional material that an educator would present in front of a classroom. Well, for Heaven's sake, he does want to become a teacher, doesn't he! The anger is replaced with salubrious, salutations proclaiming the new omnipotence of the brave new world of public education: "All he once knew and believed was now gone, and in its place was hope, wonder, and a world of information and education waiting for him." Just like Martin Luther five-hundred years ago, he was ready to nail his 99 demands to the nearest Catholic Church's parish door: "At fourteen, Patrick renounced his ties to the Catholic religion and began a High school education funded by the City of New York. " In his mind's eye, the stars in the sky were now shining brightly, their luster revealing to him the truth he had been looking for: "Suddenly, gaps in North American as well as World History left vacant in Catholic funded textbooks, had been filled, and not with nonsense, but with facts back be evidence."

However, now an adult, having had his public college educational experience at the College of Staten Island, Patrick is ready to throw in the towel, and become an Agnostic: "this is when I experienced the major difference between my high school and college.

While New Dorp's directors are almost entirely made up of former teachers, CSI's directors are mostly bureaucrats that may know to run a business, but have no idea how to run an institution." Cynicism is now rampant: "Everything from student parking, to registering for classes, to graduating on time seems to be purposely made difficult for the student." Boy, can I identify with that.

It was quite amusing to me that you wound up working as a nursing assistant, since you started your story talking about an accident that ended in a copious amount of blood and numerous stitches. Perhaps you embarked on this journey unconscious of your early realization that you are only human. It seems that now you are helping those who are realizing that they, too, are not indestructible.

Patrick Slyman's educational experience is intriguing and illustrative. He went to Catholic School. Through his experience he did not feel challenged enough. He believed they taught him from one point of view. The Catholic School taught from their own religious view. Patrick went to public school and felt he was learning from all different perspectives. He had teachers who had different outlooks. So everything for Patrick was not black and white. He was able to finally see color and life in his education according to the writing of Patrick. However from what I have read Patrick did not start his education in the Public school. I did not start my education in a Catholic School but I believe religion and faith is of great importance. The Public School for me is narrow because of its lack of faith, its lack of religion and that's why the Catholic School does have significant value. Patrick is one of those students that the Catholic School did not impact effectively or in the purpose that the institution intended. The Public School and the Catholic School both sound identical when comparing both of them. The Catholic School teaches in a limited fashion and so does the Public School. Although Patrick felt he was receiving life in the education of the Public School, others who have attended public school since day one may feel very different. Sometimes the time span of being in a certain educational institution sheds more light on the very problems within it. The way I see it New Schools need to be invented, new methods and a whole new approach needs to be implemented in the educational system. Faith should be shown in schools. Religion should be brought up in schools, also for historical purposes. Honestly I believe Public School is wrong for its approach toward religion more than anything else. The public school does not want God or anything that has to do with religion taught. This is important when learning about history. So they feed the children what they feel is appropriate. I think this is big mistake. So the stories the children learn in history at a young age are a little bit fabricated. The Catholic School might not be fulfilling its purpose but I believe the intended purpose is significant and full of value. The problem that Patrick brings up about the Catholic School is interesting but it leaves me with this one question, is the Catholic School fulfilling its purpose?

I can relate to Patrick's critique of the Catholic education system, and I did so in my own paper. We both realized that something wasn't right while in these institutions. I think he deals with the sensitive subject with great respect, while providing the solid facts that Catholic education isn't giving the whole story.

Patrick, I was shocked and horrified by your assertion that the books a materials used during your time at St. Ann's were somehow in correct, fabricated or biased. Having been the product of some thirteen years of Catholic education, I can honestly say I had a totally opposite experience and thus, am a huge proponent of the Catholic school system.

On the other hand, I do completely agree with your critique of the organizational bodies at CSI. The advisement system is chaotic, information is scattered and many staff and faculty are misinformed about requirements. Sometimes I doubt whether anybody actually knows the up-to-date information. While CSI does possess some impressive resources - like access to many internships and fellowships - it will never be taken seriously if the bureaucratic side of things is not more efficiently organized.

CHAPTER 12:
TERENCE SULLIVAN

The Education of Terence P.

Upon reflecting on my finished essay I have come to the belief that education is so much more than the acquisition of degrees or a prerequisite like an apprenticeship you must complete to have an advantage in your first job. To me education is something intrinsically more. With the aid of formal academia and the exposure to a variety of cultures, ideas, histories, the classics in literature, music, and art, all play a critical part in my development.

I am a full generation older than my classmates and I can see that the value of a college degree is so much more than a degree. Having taken classes that were either required by the college or selected by myself, I feel that a void in my understanding of life has begun to be filled. As a student of history and a historian, having access to classes that I found interesting and the new knowledge that I acquired help shape my understanding of a subject that I love. I often question if it was worth the time, effort and financial sacrifices I made on behalf of my educational pursuits. I can say unquestionably that it is.

I have found that being among like-minded students whose enthusiasm and perspectives challenged me and forced me to listen, something that I rarely did before. I realize that there is immense talent that is documented in my fellow students' essays. Everyone has a story to tell that is no less important than my own and as I read their essays I critique myself as to what have I learned from each different essay. There is always something new for me to hold on to and learn.

Through the affordability and access to the College of Staten Island my hope for a college degree will finally be realized. The faculty at the college offered

me the opportunity to explore the many facets of education and they challenged me to achieve whatever personal best I set for myself. I am profoundly indebted to the students with whom I have shared my journey with at CSI. They fed my appetite for knowledge as much as any professor. Through reflection on my own essay I have come to this truth.
T.S.

What is education? Is it the exclusive domain of academia? Perhaps it is much more than the pursuit of degrees, classes, and titles attached to your name, indicating completion of a specific course of study. Education is so much more to Terence. Terence sees his education as a constant throughout his life; evolving and shaping him into an educated man.

Terence's education has been greatly influenced by his family, and predominantly his mother. Mom had an almost religious belief in the value of education. Being number six in line of seven siblings, the path of education in the conventional sense was etched in stone. The path was cleared, and the direction was navigated through excellence in scholastic achievement, by his siblings. Terence chose a path uncharted and set a course that eventually has led him back to a traditional academic endeavor and a Bachelor's Degree.

Terence was not interested or engaged in his primary or a good part of his secondary education. His education as a young boy was culled through a series of events in his life. These events seemed to be taking place on the periphery of his life, and appeared unimpressive and unimportant. These seemingly inconsequential events have shaped his education and the essence of who he was becoming.

His mother believed that all of her children have the same level of intelligence, and their potential was equal to the next. She was especially concerned with Terence, and his lack of interest in grammar school. He hated reading. At that time in education, much was being made of Dyslexia; his mother suspected he might be afflicted. His older siblings won academic accolades as well as scholarships to high schools and universities. Yet his mother believed all her children were equally gifted and something had to be wrong with Terence. He just plugged along heading in a direction unknown to him, much less to his mother and family.

At the height of the Vietnam War, the war landed in his house. The draft would affect two of his brothers; the word lottery had an ominous meaning to Terence as a ten-year boy. He could lose both brothers with the outcome, either by war or by flight. The notion of Conscientious Objector, Canada, Nixon, McGovern, and politics, all were batted about his house, seemingly oblivious to him.

His mother was a strong advocate for the vote and how it could effect change, especially during those times. She was confined to a wheelchair and sentenced to live her life as a shut-in, yet her absentee ballot came every Election Day. As a devout Catholic, she voted Right to Life down the line. At seventeen Terence was already aware that the League of Women's Voters was where he should register to enter the political process at eighteen.

Terence's mother was a firm believer in the value of a Catholic education, and he went to a Catholic High School, Power Memorial Academy. Irish Christian Brothers were the order that taught at Power. His older brother was on scholarship, a senior as well as school president, when Terence entered as a freshman. No scholarships for him, one of seven, a dad who worked as an N.Y.P.D. patrolman. Terence paid his tuition through a paper route. Fortunately for him it was the cheapest parochial school in the city at the time.

Delivering close to a hundred papers a day, each with the headline exposed, Terence's paper route may explain why he read the news from the front to back at an early age. While his peers in high school read the news in an opposite direction, sports first, never seeming to get to the front. This always puzzled him. He remembered when the men landed on the moon; Nixon resigns, as well as the haunting image of the naked Vietnamese child fleeing napalm from American planes. As he delivered each paper the headlines made their way into his soul. This may answer why he read the paper from front to back and why he has a passion for politics and world affairs.

His high school years were quite uneventful in regard to any significant academic gains in education, though he was impressed with two teachers: Brother Jensen and Mr. Grimmeyer.

Brother Jensen taught Algebra I, as well as Greek Mythology. Terence was more impacted by the manner of the man and his ability to command attention and respect from his classes. His knowledge of the material was exceptional. Brother Jensen had a habit of wearing short-sleeved black shirts with his white collar, out of the shirt his biceps were comparable to any lineman in the N.F.L. Every boy in the school respected the raw power that was imagined he was capable of releasing. Brother Jensen was the first black man Terence had ever met; his soft-spoken manner was in stark contrast to his physique. Brother Jensen understood the nuances that came with the ages of his students. He was able to bring a racially diverse class to a level of understanding and education one would have thought impossible. He was able to engage every student on a personal level without condescension or disrespect.

It wasn't until his junior year that Mr. Grimmeyer was Terence's teacher in history. Mr. Grimmeyer's passion for the subject hadn't dulled over time and his enthusiasm was contagious. Terence was astonished to learn that Mr. Grimmeyer was investigated by the F.B.I. for having a Soviet magazine, *Soviet Life*, delivered to him from the Soviet Union every month. Mr. Grimmeyer's concentration of study was Russian History. Terence enjoyed that class, and was fascinated with the complexities of history presented by Mr. Grimmeyer.

The natural progression for his family after high school was college, with the exception of Terence. Terence made the decision to join the military after high school. His mother was concerned having lived through the torture of envisioning sons on the battlefields of Vietnam. She and his older brothers viewed his enlistment with complete disbelief. His mother never asked him not to go, yet she had registered Terence for Saint Francis College in the fall, just in case. The importance of education to his mother was always evident.

Terence and his friend were to join the Marines together; his friend was definitely Marine material and the reality was that Terence wasn't. Terence decided on the Air Force. The toughest decision of his young life came on the day he was to leave for basic training. What was promised to him by the recruiter could not be guaranteed. He went to the phone booth and dialed home; with the intent of asking his mom what he should do. After the last number was dialed he hung up. It was time for Terence to grow up and make his own decisions. He left for basic training mid-November 1978.

Terence expected to gain the discipline and control through military service that could transform him into a better student. The military he hoped would make him more focused and ready to follow the well-traveled path of education known so well to his siblings. He was surprised to find out that he had no adjustment problems, even though there were two attempted suicides in his platoon the first few days. Terence was baffled why these boys would attempt to kill themselves. He thought about it. Maybe being in basic training through Thanksgiving, Christmas and New Year's wasn't the most ideal time to join. Nevertheless he fared well.

From basic training he went to technical school for avionic communications training in Biloxi, Mississippi. Being brought up in Brooklyn, Terence suffered a serious case of culture shock being in the South. Some of the people he met seemed to be still fighting the Civil War in their prejudices and attitudes. Terence was not an activist, so he just trudged on getting along with everyone. Terence thought about tolerance and perhaps his tolerance was born at home. It served him well.

Technical school was a blur, electronic theory, more math, formulas, algebra; he couldn't escape education, even in the military. Terence was able to perform marginally well enough to graduate after six months. He became a communications "mechanic" while his classmates were what they were trained for, "technician." Terence received orders and was sent to Nebraska, SAC Headquarters. Being geographically challenged he first believed he was headed to Nevada and Las Vegas. No such luck.

In Nebraska he was well liked and performed his job and duties with excellence. Terence received numerous meritorious awards and accolades. The primary mission of the base was a 24/7 aerial command post with nuclear launch capabilities. He was given the midnight shift to run. Terence was given the opportunity to deploy to England and assist in the "Looking Glass" operations as support for reconnaissance aircraft. He saw first-hand what was considered our number one enemy, the Soviets. His mission was under the exclusive oversight of the Joint Chiefs of Staff and the Pentagon, which explains why he lived in a small hotel with maid service in rural England. It was quite a memorable experience for him.

After four years of service and being honorably discharged, Terence learned he had received an associate's degree from the Community College of the Air Force. Within one month of being discharged he got a job doing clerical work, with an international bank. He was glad to have found something so soon. Having free time in the evenings Terence enrolled in Kingsborough Community College, and took random classes like drawing, tennis, and a history class in Twentieth Century America.

The next four years Terence had a series of different jobs, never being satisfied where he was. He applied for, and was accepted into the apprentice program of the electricians union. His honorable discharge, the suit and tie he wore, and the respect he learned at home got him accepted.

The apprentice program required Terence to go to classes twice a week, four hours a night for four plus years, while working a full day in construction. He was beginning to realize that education was going to be a constant in his life. The union weeded out those who weren't willing to toe the line and apprentices were dropped from the program regularly. The program required two hours of electric theory on all systems having to do with commercial and residential electrical installations. The next two hours professors from Empire State College taught a curriculum of core and labor studies. Upon completion of the apprenticeship program Terence received an Associate's Degree in Labor Studies. His political indoctrination into unionism had begun.

For twenty-three years of cyclical employment in construction, Terence continued his education during these slow periods. He began taking courses at Saint Francis College, mostly history. Terence gained a measure of confidence when a professor singled him out for a paper he felt had the strongest content. Terence realized that he was as capable as other students meeting the challenges of college. This incident convinced him that perhaps he was indeed college material. Academic pursuits fell from the forefront of Terence's aspirations, for a while. Life got in the way, marriage, home with a mortgage, and the blessings of children, contributed immeasurably to his education while academic pursuits became less important to him through these years.

After years of crawling up and down thirty stories of steel, his trade took its toll on him physically and Terence retired. He returned to school. Terence had chosen CSI to continue his pursuit of an education. Terence heard good things from some young graduates he knew. Upon entering CSI, Terence was listed as junior and chose History as his major. In the spring of 2010 he enrolled in three History classes: Hist. 218 (The Roman World), 386 (Recovery of Women's Past), 200 (Historical Method). It never occurred to Terence that being away from college so long, that the workload would be daunting. It was. The Roman history class was enlightening; he never had a working understanding of the Roman Empire; and it filled a void he had not realized existed. Historical Methods helped him in further understanding historical perspectives of historians and the many differing ways History is chronicled. The Recovery class was by far the toughest. The workload was impossible; ten book reviews, essays, papers, and finals. His very first paper was returned with an "NG" and a comment that it was not college material and to redo it. Professor Cooper suggested that he ask to see someone else's paper to compare. He struggled through the essay for a second, third, even a fourth time and received a C-. This was one of the lowest grades he had received for the amount of work he felt he did.

Terence found everything he felt that a college professor should be in Professor Cooper, brilliant, knowledgeable, and she set the bar of excellence extremely high. Terence had difficulty adjusting to the strict demands of the class. Terence approached Professor Cooper to discuss his concerns in meeting her requirements of the course. Professor Cooper unequivocally assured him that he belonged in her class. She welcomed older students, saying that his presence assured that the "monkey business" of immature students could wane significantly with the addition of serious minded students. By the time of the mid-term half of the original class had dropped. He began to quake. Sandi Cooper expected much out of her students, especially history majors, and she got it from Terence. He was engaged by her lectures; and at times felt that she was privately tutoring him. Professor Cooper welcomed all his questions, which he was constantly firing at her. He had much to learn from her. Being in her class afforded him the privilege of being challenged on a personal level and meeting her high standards.

In the fall of 2010 Terence entertained the idea of teaching high school, so he applied and was accepted to the education program. His courses this semester were EDS 202 (Psychological Foundations of Secondary Education), HIST 300 (Historiography), and HIST 222 (Islam: Religion and Culture). The education class was interesting to Terence. He has two daughters in high school and it helped his understanding of the educational hurdles they were encountering. He had taken an education course years ago at Saint Francis, and topics taught then were also covered here, so he did well.

As a witness to the murders of innocents on 9/11, and seeing the collapse of the Twin Towers, the rage toward all things Middle Eastern flowed through his very essence. Terence fed and nourished his rage and his intolerance reached a new level. The only N.Y.P.D. female officer murdered, Moira Reddy Smith, was a dear friend. The majority of his friends are cops and firemen. After months of working twelve-hour shifts in the acrid smoldering pile, they each went to where Moira was last seen to work on their own time and searched for her. Never has a man been blessed with friends as he was.

Years later Terence was compelled to gain an understanding of Islam. He felt that this course would help in being less intolerant and more knowledgeable. The professor teaching the course Terence found to be the most arrogant, biased, opinionated, and message driven person he had ever met.

He was in the minority ethnic dynamic of the class, and was the subject of ridicule, and his opinions dismissed. Terence was stunned she was an educator. Terence had remembered years ago that a fundamental and universal ideal of "Academic Freedom"; loosely translated: it was the free exchange of ideas and opinions that were the foundation of collegiate pursuits. Sadly this did not exist in his Hist. 222 class. In spite of her, Terence gained insight into Islam and Middle Eastern culture primarily through the interaction of younger classmates, and completing the assigned reading. In the spring of 2011, his personal life became complicated and Terence only took Hist. 340 (U.S. Foreign Policy). This class opened his eyes to view American Foreign Policy more as a realist and no longer as an idealist.

In the fall of 2011 Terence took PSY 100 (Psychology), MTH 020 (A no credit remedial math class), and HST 339 (U.S. History Themes 1914-1945). That semester opened his eyes to the inadequacies of entry-level classes. Terence was now taking two freshmen classes and he experienced the stark difference in maturity compared with the other classes he took. The drama in these classes seemed to continue all semester unabated. He was accustomed to like-minded students with similar interests. It was difficult for him to have any connection between these students and the ones that he had in all of his previous classes.

Terence took the math class to see if at this stage of his life, he could master the analytical content that had always seemed to elude him. No such luck. This class he felt was a disgrace; students who could not grasp the concepts in high school were now thrown into a required class that contained absolutely no instruction or explanation. How could a college expect a student to successfully pass a class that was devoid of any in-class instruction? Terence could see this as a real moneymaker for the college. He bought an on-line program that was required, and did repetition exercises on line, and in class more of the same. Terence got a pass in this class, more importantly he came to the realization that he did not have the analytical gifts of his siblings. Terence was more philosophical by nature. He accepted that fact with no negative implications or feelings of inferiority. It's who he is.

History 339 was one of his favorite classes. The Professor incorporated a vast amount of New York History in this course and Terence had a keen interest. His final research paper was rich with primary sources and the professor commented on how good they were. The professor's grading of the final paper, he had heard from other students, was tough, so he kept his grade to himself. Terence received an A as his final grade. Terence attributes his competence in research to the rich lessons learned in historiography at CSI. Terence enjoys helping his two daughters who are in high school, finding convincing sources and how to differentiate between acceptable sources for their papers in history.

Asked to think of someone he considers to be an educated person, Terence made an unlikely choice, his arch nemesis as a child, his best friend Walter's younger brother Kevin. Kevin was the youngest of a gifted family; some of those gifts were very rare, such as decency, respect, a sense of fairness and compassion. When Kevin and Terence's paths crossed when they were in grade school, the antagonism would begin. Kevin would lob insults at him, usually having to do with his size and fueled by his older sister's vast use of Webster's Thesaurus providing synonyms for "fat" for Kevin. The good Lord saw fit to give Kevin the gift of speed, always keeping Kevin a safe arm's length from Terence.

Kevin remained off Terence's radar while he was in the Air Force. Kevin was away at college pursuing his direction in life. Walter and Terence cemented a lasting relationship as best friends during those years. When Terence and Walter got together, the occasional mention of Kevin kept Terence relatively informed of Kevin's pursuits. Terence felt that Kevin's pursuits sounded more like escapades.

By chance Terence ran into Kevin years later in a diner in midtown. Kevin was there in an N.Y.P.D. uniform. As was Terence's custom whenever he saw a cop, he would look to see if it was someone he knew or if the cop knew any of his friends in that precinct. As he entered the diner he first saw the uniform. It looked awfully big on this young cop. Terence's line of vision settled on the face. It was a familiar face with barely any facial hair, and to Terence seemed out of place to be wrapped in an N.Y.P.D.

uniform. Then it registered with Terence this young cop before him was Kevin. Kevin was no longer the adversary of childhood, he was a rookie cop. Terence saw Kevin in a new light and a new found respect for the man. Terence felt that a mutual respect for each other took hold by the end of their brief conversation.

Kevin attended many different colleges before he finally graduated with his bachelor's. Terence was surprised that Kevin was going for his law degree at New York Law School, while working full time as a cop. Kevin's aspirations contributed to Terence's decision to finish his degree. Kevin successfully finished law school, all the while maintaining a balance with his job, family and home.

As the years passed, Kevin's second child developed a form of cancer at a very young age. Having two children of his own Terence could only imagine how tormented Kevin's life must have felt. Terence was kept abreast of Kevin's daughter's progress when speaking with Walter. Kevin's little girl beat the cancer thankfully, and Kevin forged ahead with the balancing act of family and career.

Kevin is driven by a career and city he loves, yet he never sacrificed his core principles, that family and friends were first and last. Kevin rose through the ranks of the N.Y.P.D. Kevin's education culminated with a master's degree in Public Administration from Harvard's Kennedy School. Terence was immensely proud of Kevin and his academic accomplishments.

Terence gained insight into how their relationship had changed over time. At the annual Christmas dinner; where childhood friends got together, Kevin delivered a toast to friendship; he signaled out Walter and Terence as having the longest friendship of the group. Terence realized that they held identical convictions of friends and family.

Political discussions with Kevin were always an opportunity for Terence to gain insight into opposing political viewpoints. Terence was in the political minority among his friends. Kevin demanded that if Terence were to engage into political discussions with him he needed to be prepared. Kevin was always prepared to argue the conservative position with Terence, and Terence would argue the "Conservative Democratic" position with Kevin. ("Conservative Democratic" is not part of Kevin's vernacular.) Kevin would never dismiss Terence's point of view; rather Kevin remained even-tempered and continued to point counter-point with Terence.

Kevin would never miss a chance to label Terence as a "liberal zealot" in jest. At one time Terence had his youngest daughter register in a very promising public high school, only to find out after four weeks she was on the receiving end of racial abuse by other students. Terence pulled her out and sent her back to Catholic school. Kevin remarked that in the future if Terence were to engage in liberal experimentation, not to include his children. Terence found this remark truly thought-provoking when said by someone he was comfortable with.

Terence heard of an incident that Kevin was involved in within the N.Y.P.D. A childhood friend was under investigation by the internal affairs department. This guy was in serious trouble. Kevin's position in the department was on an increasingly upward course when he was called in and questioned about his meeting with this childhood friend. Kevin told them that he was not turning his back on his friend, especially when a friend needed him most. Many ambitious careers are made at the expense of friendships, and loyalties are cast aside as inconvenient. Kevin remained steadfast in his loyalty by giving his friend advice as to his best options. Guilt by association never caused Kevin to waiver, he never compromised his convictions, and his career in the N.Y.P.D. got right back on track. There is no doubt that Kevin has the credentials of education, yet Terence found the qualities he admired most about Kevin were the same qualities that do not always come with a formal education. Terence sees this as the essence of an educated man.

One More Thought . .

Finally in a comparison with Henry Adams, Terence found Adams driven by education throughout his life. Adams judged the worth of education by

whether he gained anything through his experiences. Adams is critical of most of his experiences in life as having no educational value. Terence sees all experiences in life as educational. Even what appears to be of no use has value. The most seemingly insignificant insight into both a negative and a positive experience has educational value to Terence. In recalling an episode of "All in the Family", Archie Bunker was condescending to a mentally challenged character. Throughout the show Archie was meticulously pointing out the challenged characters many handicaps and dismissing all he had to say. The show culminated with the closing remark from this character to Archie "Every man is my superior in that I may learn from him." We should always consider that we could learn something from the most unsuspected person as long as we don't assume that we are better than them. By treating everyone as our equal we are less likely to miss an opportunity to learn through his or her eyes. This memory of the show and in particular that remark has stayed with Terence for much of his adult life, he believes that it is a sound view to take in the ongoing process of becoming educated.
T.S.

TERENCE'S CLASSMATES RESPOND

Although we are of a different religion, I see some significant similarities between us. We are both white, working class, blue-collar types who were raised in the same era of the 60's and 70's. We both had educational aspirations that we hoped would help us "rise above" our blue-collared backgrounds. We had a desire to learn and acquire the knowledge education offered to us, in spite of the stereotype of our socio-economic background. I too was in the Air Force, stationed in South Jersey, while on leave from my job with the City of New York. It's uncanny that I have learned the same thing that Terrance did, especially as it refers to my job, which is: "By treating everyone as our equal we are less likely to miss an opportunity to learn through his or her eyes."

The Education of Terence P. illustrates a man determined to reach his goal of achieving his bachelor's degree. He believes that no matter what the experience of the educational system, whether bad or good he is still learning. He is still receiving an education. Education to Terrence never ends because he believes it is an ongoing journey. This I agree with, education has no limits. Education continues throughout our entire life. I do stand firmly with my position that it does matter whether the experience of education is bad or good. Terrence was able to say "I will use whatever experience I have and make it work for me." This is wonderful but some students cannot get back up when they get knocked down. Sometimes the negative educational experience is an on-going journey that needs to end. Sometimes students get one bad teacher after another and though they know their teachers are unacceptable "who can they run to to tell on these kinds of teachers?" it is a situation that needs to be taken care of immediately. Terrence is much older than his classmates but we all have so much in common. Terrence states "I realize that there is immense talent that is documented in my fellow student's essays. Everyone has a story to tell that is no less important than my own and as I read their essays I critique myself as to what have I learned from each different essay. There is always something new for me to hold on to and learn." He has an awareness of not just himself but others. Terrence is humble and has a hunger for learning. His educational experience teaches all of us a lesson that life changes and people change.

Terence is living proof that you can go to school but you can't buy class. He is a gentleman and a scholar and is shaped by his life experience and brings it into everyday aspects in any situation he is in. Having other older students in my classes before, many of them seemed annoyed by the younger students whenever they asked a question that had been answered or was obvious. Terence realizes that everyone learns at different paces and rather than be quick to judge them, he listens to their story and tries to see where they are coming from which takes time and patience. Your kids should read your paper, they have a cool dad.

Terence's story is bountiful with learning experiences. He has never "settled" and instead chooses to continue learning until he can find a career that he is truly passionate about. He is also able to use his military career as a foundation for his future success which not a lot of people take advantage of.

Terence, your academic and worldly education sound like it has been quite an adventure thus far. It was amazing to read of your journey--from living at home among six other brothers and sisters, having a teacher suspected of being a communist by the FBI, to the military and having a family, along with a growing relationship with your friend's brother, Kevin. What is the most interesting aspect of your education is that there is more than what you have chosen to write here! After all, one must be selective when writing a certain number of pages about their whole life/education!

Kudos to you, Terence, for coming back and finishing your degree. I admire your steadfast determination to be educated, expand your horizons and expel ignorance throughout your life. As I progress along life's path I hope I have the wherewithal and humility to resolve my gaps in knowledge with the same poise and industry that you have shown.

I also I agree with you on several counts. First, I am also more philosophical than analytical. Secondly, the remedial math classes are disgraceful and definitely a scam! Finally, I am equally happy that you share a positive view of a traditional Catholic education!

CHAPTER 13:
CRYSTAL TALBOT

"We Plan God Laughs" is a narrative written by Crystal M. Talbert. The piece is a reflection on the various paths of her life's course. Her writing reveals a bumpy road to self- discovery, love and self-actualization in her role as a mother. The positive air in the writing combined with thoughtful anecdotes of her life's ironic moments, reinforces the principle that "everything happens for a reason." The author used her positive outlook and her effort to see the glass half full as a reoccurring theme to guide her writing. Her story highlights the importance of self-discovery and the ability to remain grounded, positive, flexible and above all faithful to religious convictions. She states "through day to day life faith alone is what motivates me in all aspects."
C.T

WE PLAN ... GOD LAUGHS

As humans much of our lives are determined by our surroundings and the people around us. For me, much of my life played out according to who raised me and how they chose to do it. Other factors in my young adult education were affected by the schools I went to, the company I kept and my desire to fit into mainstream American society. Now, from the point of view of a wife and mother, I can examine my educational path and my social choices.

As a Catholic I was taught at a very young age, "your path in life is predetermined before you are born." At age seventeen my mother Gloria emigrated from Belize is search of a better life. She followed her soon to be husband, my father Glen, because he came to America looking for opportunities to become a business owner. My parents' choice to come to America deeply affected their lives and shaped the lives of their children. Growing up in a Belizean household, surrounded by an American society, played a large role in how I perceived the world.

My brothers attended parochial school from pre-k through twelfth grade in a Belizean tradition of private education. After my parents divorced in 1994, my mother was unable to sustain the cost of private education for my sisters and me, just starting kindergarten. She also felt that public schools had more to offer in extracurricular activities and after school programs.

In middle school I attended William A. Morris School for the Performing Arts in the theater and dance programs. The program selected students by application and audition only. My love for the arts truly blossomed during my middle school years.

I had a very concertedly cultivated life which consisted of going to school with regular classes as well as three extra electives, theater, stage craft, and dance. After school I also participated in the musicals, and as a varsity member of the dance team, and in my last year was awarded the position of Captain.

After those activities I also attended Staten Island Ballet (SIB), and took part in their annual performance of the Nutcracker which took up my weekends along with church and CCD. Summers were no different. I was always occupied with performing arts camps and community theater programs as well as an intensive summer dance program at SIB.

In High School I chose not to continue pursuing the performing arts path, despite my longing for it. I auditioned for La Guardia High School of Preforming arts in eighth grade only to be rejected. Rejection was difficult. I could only rationalize the rejection by blaming my physical appearance and body type as the cause for failure. I began to hate myself.

I had the chance to audition again the next year, but realized that I did not want to stress myself out with going into the city every day for a specialized school, only to be told after four years that I wasn't tall enough or skinny enough. This decision was a reflection of a negative body image perpetuated by rejection and disappointment. Studying dance taught me to be very body conscious. I didn't like what I saw, and I was bordering on an eating disorder. I was quite aware of my issues, and I knew how to fix it. I never even tried.

High school was the time when things fluctuated a lot for m. I went through what my mom calls the beginning of my depression because of my identity issues that began with my body. I chose to stop dancing and I began not to care about my school work, and I was eventually taken out of my honors program. All I cared about was friends, and hanging out with who was popular. I did pick up track and soccer, two things that I briefly did in elementary school. I come from a very athletic family, so it wasn't typical of what you might think when a dancer goes out for sports. I excelled here as well, because I wasn't so wrapped up in my own things. I was more involved with my peers.

I learned of things like peer pressure and cliques. I never realized that while I was involved with the performing arts so much, I never really had one group of friends. I knew everyone and vice versa, but only as Crystal "the dancer girl" or the lead in the play, not as Crystal the normal teenager trying to find out who she is amongst everyone else. This realization caused many feuds between me and the girls who were once my friends. I came to find out that while I was excelling in dance and theater they were jealous of me. I never acted as though I was above anyone, but this jealousy still resulted. These sentiments from them definitely showed up once I threw myself into their world of the normal teen. I rebelled. I began to skip practices and found new friends on the other side of the Island. Now all I was interested in was hanging out with them every day and being with my boyfriend.

Those friendships never lasted long, and I was always having to find new groups, and it kept getting worse and worse. I began to cut classes, but I would show up for tests and hand in bulk assignments that I had missed and yet to the astonishment of my teachers I would pass with C's; of course I couldn't receive Bs because I had missed so much class. I was always being lectured on how smart I was and how I had so much potential, but it only pushed me away more. That was the old me, which was based on the security of the arts I had formerly been rooted in. But I didn't have that anymore, so why should I care about my grades? My mom saw where I was headed and decided that I should spend a summer in Kansas with my brother, who was in the Air Force. So, I did, and I loved the idea of a new start so much that I decided to stay there and finish high school.

My Kansas High School experience was much better than when I started in Staten Island. I did better with grades and even made it back into some honors classes, but I of course got lazy and by the end of junior year, those Cs started showing up again. My brother was very hard on me, and forced me to quit soccer because of my grades. His strictness also showed through house work and curfews. I always pushed the limits with him, and even if I was late ten minutes I was in big trouble.

Then came senior year, and I had a very light schedule of about two classes per day. In Kansas there is a different way of attending school and the duration of the time spent in each class. School was according to a block schedule were you had "black days" and "white days" (named after our school colors). This is where we attended only four classes per day (instead of eight like in NY) and the time spent in those classes was doubled. My classes were being an office aide, teacher's assistant, history and seminar. For the seminar I decided to take the community service option, which allowed me not to have to go to a class. Instead I would need to volunteer in the city for credit.

Towards the end of the semester I began to slack on my hours near the end and scrambled to find volunteer work. This meant that I had to skip my history class a time or two. However, in Kansas when you miss school without a note or call from your guardian, the school calls your home. And I was slick, I had given the school my cell number in case I missed a class, therefore I would get the call and not my brother or sister-in-law. But for some reason they called my old number, and my brother found out. I tried to explain it to him, but he didn't care for an excuse. This was too much for me, because I felt like he was an authoritarian rather than just authoritative. I decided that moving in with my boyfriend and his family was better for me.

Moving to Kansas was a profound moment in my life which did help to resolve my major problems, but of course I still made mistakes along the way. But something good that came out of all of my high school years was the love for each one of my history teachers. I don't have a bad memory of any of them. This, although I did not realize it at the time, would directly affect my college decisions, and put me on the path that I am on today.

Once college decisions started to fill the air I had the choice to stay in Kansas or come back to Staten Island. I had great opportunities to major in dance at two colleges in Kansas, on scholarship, but ultimately I missed New York, and a spring break trip back here only reaffirmed my homesickness for New York. Therefore I decided to come back and attend CSI as a nursing student. I did very well in my first semester but once I got to the Anatomy part of the degree I realized that it wasn't for me. I realized that I was doing it for the "good money" nursing could get me. I began to ponder what I really wanted to do, and I recalled my love for all of my history teachers. That was when I switched my degree to history.

At CSI I have taken many different types of courses. I have never limited myself to taking easy electives. This is also in part because of my first year as a nursing major. Having taken different courses I have also encountered different professors. Some I have not liked at all and was in a constant feud with, and others were just a joy to have. I feel that neither bad nor good experiences with professors at CSI have shaped me. The only thing that really had an effect on me was that horrific Anatomy class, which I don't think was the professor's fault at all.

I also feel that in college it is important that no matter what class you take there is something for you to learn. You must stay open minded as a college student, and even if it is only one thing, that is more than others might be able to say. I know that I can honestly say that whether a course was directly relevant or not to my degree, I have taken little bits from each one that I have always remembered, and that will be plain old knowledge for me in everyday life. I believe that I am a more knowledgeable person because of each class that I have taken, and that even makes me a better historian.

My history classes are the same as the core classes that I have taken, all of them focusing on different time periods and ideas. In these history classes I have liked some and disliked others, yet I have taken at least something out of each, whether conscious or unconsciously.

As I mentioned before I had a boyfriend in Kansas. He ended up moving back to Staten Island with me and he proposed a couple of years after and we got married one year after that on April 10th, 2010. Two months after our marriage we found out that we were expecting our first child and were about a month along. This was exciting yet scary news. We hadn't been actively trying to get pregnant. We were following Natural Family Planning to hold off pregnancy for a couple years. But as my faith teaches me, whatever is meant to be is going to happen. My faith is something that I came to rely on heavily through the pre-marriage classes we took. It helped me to understand why things happen and to just know that there is a plan in place for me, and it is my job to be aware of that and try to follow it to the best of my ability.

Through my new-found faith, I was able to move past the former devastation of my dancing years, and troubled times that followed and find other facets for my creativity and talents. I learned to accept dance in any form that I can take part in, whether it be teaching or just watching. Dance still captures my mind whenever a great tune hits the radio, but I do not dwell on what might have been if I had continued down a professional route. I learned to be satisfied with what I do have, instead of what I might lack. This notion and the fact that I was now a wife and soon to be mother, led me to find my love for crafting and being the best wife and mother I could be. These things I found satisfy me because I always knew I ultimately wanted to be these things. It just happened a bit sooner than I would have expected.

I came to accept the past, and welcome the future with whatever it might bring. I have learned that education is not necessarily just something in the formal sense, but a reference to life experiences, since life is a complete learning experience. I now "live and learn," a quote that not only helps me accept life, but keeps my faith strong at the same time knowing that one mistake or change is not the end. This is something I ultimately was taught and learned from my mother, which I most likely failed to hear in my adolescent years. I consider her to be one of the most highly educated persons in my life, because she "lives and learns," and she has taught me some valuable lessons that I will always carry with me. My mother ultimately gave me the best education that I could have received and this was one that made sure to connect me with my faith, and this makes it the only true education that will always matter and can never be truly judged by any other human.

From the point of view of a wife and mother I have been able to see my overall educational experience as rich and meaningful. I have learned much from my formal education in college and that experience will always stay with me. But I have learned more from my life experiences through faith, my upbringing and my experiences as a mother and wife. My life experiences are priceless lessons that I would not trade for any formal education. They are what shaped me into the person I am today and the culmination of my experiences have provided a platform for fruitful life experiences and further learning to continue.

C.T.

CRYSTAL'S CLASSMATES RESPOND

With a title of "We Plan…God Laughs," I thought the theme would have religious significance. Her elementary and Junior high school experiences were the happiest time of her life, until recently, when she married and had a child. There was a time when she was a dancer, which she took so much pleasure while participating in because of her natural ability. Then she spent the rest of her adolescence rebelling against all authority, the preponderance of which were the school authorities. She did everything she could to spend as little time as possible in the classroom. Her brother was right in not wanting to tolerate her truancy. After High School, her rebelliousness gradually gave way to complacency and non-judgmental acceptance of the status quo.

What better way to absolve oneself of rebellion, than to assume the mantle of faithful obedience to one's religion. Of course, the Catholic Church is famous for blind faith. You have no control of your life because God has a plan for you: "to just know that there is a plan in place for me." Although you profess to, "the importance of self-discovery," religious orthodoxy only wants you to discover yourself within their own narrow minded dogma. "But as my fate teaches me, whatever is meant to be is going to be."

I'm sorry, but I believe in controlling as much of my life as I can. In my religious beliefs, Jesus does not want me to blindly believe in the status quo. I do believe he wants me to love one another, as you would love yourself.

If I may turn to more pleasant thoughts, like you, I too still have fond memories of Kansas. I still occasionally visit friends in that area. Topeka is a really nice small sized city. Happy Trails to you.

"We Plan…God Laughs," by Crystal Talbert tells the story of a rebellious girl who transforms herself into a determined woman. She loves dancing. I have seen with my own eyes one of Crystal's many talents. Let me say first hand her dancing is amazing. She believes that faith has brought her through her times of trouble and sacrifice. Crystal shares with readers that being a dancer does not define her. She shares that having the wrong friends did not define her. Crystal realized that she had to find herself, her worth and her own value. So Crystal thought, I will be a dancer, I will always have these friends but the truth for Crystal was all that she planned did not happen. Some would ask why? It is because God laughed and told Crystal "I have it all figured out."

"Live and Learn" is the perfect premise in my opinion to have in regard to our education. Crystal's culmination of life experiences, like myself, is the essence of her education. Crystal's journey helps me to understand my own daughters' journey a little better especially the "Live and Learn" part.

Clearly your faith has guided you in making many choices, which is good. I too strongly believe in my faith. As humans we should all have something we strongly believe in and it doesn't necessary have to be religious faiths. As long as you as a human know what you want out of life, even as a young teenager, it will help keep a balance between school and play but regardless of which route you take life really is about 'living and learning.'

I value the same perception of education as you. Although I'm thankful for my formal education I've learned more from my life experiences just as you. The quote live and learn in your paper has always been tattooed to the back of my hand because it's important to learn from your life experiences and mistakes.

Holy wow, this was both touching and inspiring. You wrote with such ease that the words were able to flow. This piece was deep, filled with honesty, self-criticism, identification, and responsibility. I appreciate your candor as you described your life and education that has led you to dabble in the History major. It sure sounds like Kansas was the best thing that could have happened to you!

Building on Laurie's comments, I agree that Kansas was the best thing that could've ever happened to you. I also can relate because I feel that Australia was the best thing to ever happen to me. Sometimes the experiences we have in different places can be the most educational and eye-opening!

It's very interesting that you were able to learn from two completely different schooling systems between New York and Kansas. We are similar in that it took college for us to really buckle down in school and do what was necessary.

CHAPTER 14:
DANA VECCHIARELLI

Approaching the end of my college semester I feel that I have gained a lot and am really looking forward to where I go next in my life. I feel that I have learned so much up to this point and can walk away with a great education and if I had to change it I wouldn't. It's interesting and hard at the same time to sit and write about yourself and what has motivated you and influenced you because you think about all the little things in your life that really are the big causes for helping you shape your own life. As I approach my last semester of college I stop and take a look at how far I have come and how I got to where I am today. I look back and think about all the things in my life that have made me the person I am and what influenced and motivated me the most.
D.V.

My earliest memory I have of my education is my first day of pre-school. I went to an all-girls Catholics private school. I went to the school with the same group of girls from pre-k to my senior year of high school. I loved going to pre-K, I remember, I loved my teacher. She was very hands on always interacting with the kids. I also remember snack time as my favorite time of the day.

As I got older and started first and second grade I remember that's when I started to realize I always struggled in school. I always would have extra tutor time with my teachers or need extra time with practicing my reading or math. In the school that I grew up in majority of the students were smart and really didn't struggle and when a student came along who did struggle like me, it was like a hassle or a setback for them. I always felt like I get pushed to the side and never got the one-on-one I needed with my teachers so my mom would always have extra tutors for me outside of school. That is one of the main reasons why I would like to teach myself, so I can be nothing like the teachers I had growing up. I want to help kids who struggle in school and give students the extra push and motivation that they need. I want to make sure I would never make a student feel the way I did growing up and struggling in school.

I do have early memories of where my interest in history first started. It was my kindergarten class and once a week we would have another teacher come in and teach us history. The first thing I learned in history was about Christopher Columbus. We had a song that went along with it and still remember it today. I guess that's where it all started for me was Christopher Columbus. As I got into middle school, history became one of my favorite classes. I had to do a project in the eighth grade about Ellis Island so I interviewed my grandparents about their trip here from Italy. My teacher asked me if they would come into the class and speak and discuss what it was like. My grandmother came in and I remember sitting there listening to her and thinking wow my own grandma is like a history book, she has been and seen so much. I thought it was so interesting and that was my first encounter with a real primary source.

As I started high school, history was still one of my favorite classes but I always thought the way they taught it was so boring; you would sit there and copy notes off the board. History should be more hands on, group discussions. My junior year of high school was one of my most difficult years in school. I was preparing for my SATS, regents, and school work. Over Easter vacation I got into a car accident with two friends from school that would change my life forever. I was involved in the car accident due to speeding. I was sitting in the back seat and hit my forehead. I suffered a severe concussion and I have a scar going down my forehead that I will have for the rest of my life. After that car accident I was very depressed, very insecure that I had this scar on my face and kind of lost my interest in doing school work. I had so many things going on in my head that I couldn't seem to focus on anything. I remember one day thinking to myself in life you go through struggles and hit bumps but you just need to move forward not stop and this will all pass and one day it will just be a memory and something that made you stronger. I honestly thought that to myself one day and was able to move on get back into the swing of things, focus on my school work, get into college and start the next chapter in my life.

In my senior year of high school when I started applying to colleges I remember sitting with my college advisor and she would ask me so what are your interests? What would you like to study or do when you are older? And I remember thinking to myself, I am seventeen years old, I have no idea what I want to do when I am older and really not sure yet even what I am that interested in. At the time I worked part time in a small clothing boutique and I liked fashion and I guess that was something I was interested in at the time. I am sure most other seventeen year old girls liked fashion. So I decided on Berkeley College in Manhattan and studied fashion merchandising. Long story short, totally was not interested and hated it.

Back to my issue about always struggling in school and not getting the proper help, this is an example of it in the school I went to. Because I was not a straight A student and did not score amazingly on my SATS I was not looking at Ivy League colleges so the advisors kind of just helped me get by minus the "guidance" part of their jobs. If I got better guidance in applying to schools and maybe applying to the right schools I would have found something better for me. That's where I find myself lucky enough to have caring and understanding parents who stepped in and helped me realize that going somewhere else was the best decision for me. After my freshman year of college I sat down with my parents and had a long chat with them on what I wanted to do. College was always important in my family and no matter what, I had to finish it, no ifs ands or buts. My parents let me take a semester off look into some other schools and try and figure out what I liked and what maybe I would want to study. That was probably the best thing I did because I did some research, really looked into what I enjoyed and kept finding myself going back to teaching and history.

Teaching and history were the main focus at that point. I decided to go to CSI to study what I was interested in. When I first started here I kind of had to start over, being that all I took before were fashion classes. I had to take a lot of sciences, a foreign language, and core history classes. At first I was a little uninterested because I was all ready to jump into history classes but I didn't realize I had to take all my core classes first. I needed to stay focused because I have the tendency to loss interest in something fast when I don't feel connected to a certain topic or subject, but I got through all my Spanish classes, my science and lab classes and finally made my way to all the interesting, well mostly all the interesting, history classes I wanted to take. One class sticks out to me the most that if I could take the class all over again I would in a second. It was history of Late Imperial China with Professor Lufrano. I remembered when I signed up for it; it was a Thursday night class 6:30 to 9:50 which was my first night class and 300 level class. I was dreading it. I thought to myself ugh this is so late how I will even be able to stay alert and what if I don't even like the class. Well I was wrong; the class blew me away. The way the professor taught made the class so interesting and so easy to follow him and what he was talking about. History classes can at times be very boring when you sit and just listen to a professor or teacher just lecture but he just made the class interesting with great stories, pictures that really got you into the class. I would actually look forward to his class because every time the class was over he would leave you with that feeling of you wanted to know more. When the class was over I felt like I walked away with so much new knowledge on a topic that I would probably never really think about or look into studying.

I went on and took many more history classes. I got a feel of almost every aspect of history from all over the world, from American, European, African, and even medieval history. Some classes obviously better than others and some maybe I could have even done without. When you take a step back you realize why I took so many different types of history classes. They want you to get a feel of all different types of history and maybe see what catches your interest and even areas you would never think to study like in my class late imperial China.

I do have one class in particular that I found was the most difficult for me and I really thought this class would be the reason I would not be able to get through college. It was my History 300 class. It was a very intense study of different historians and their views and ideas on certain topics, historians like Bede and Machiavelli, for example, and we would look into their works and analyze and studied them. For me I found the class very difficult and challenging which is a good thing because it forced me to think in ways that I have never done before in a history class. It was like stepping out of your comfort zone instead of just reading about it in a text book and telling about something I had to do the research and uncover what they were talking about. It just came to a point where I had no idea what I was reading and I was totally disinterested in the class. The professor was not that helpful and most of the students in the class struggled a lot.

I even find my love for history with the job I have today. I work for a company called the Frye Company; it is a US boot brand. I work in their showroom and assist with the buyers. After I started working for the company a couple months I started to look into the history of the company and wanted to know more. Turns out after doing all my research I did find a lot. It has been around since 1832, a family owned company, the first US and still the only bench crafted boot making company still in the US. I took all my information I gathered and compiled a basically history book and the company uses it today as our own little history book of Frye. I just love researching and finding new things.

A look back . . .

As I look back in the journey of my life I take a step back and really analyze everything that went on and how I feel I have been educated and have experienced so many things to get where I am today. I realized that education is a never ending process. Even though I am in my last semester of college I don't want to stop my education here. I would like to further it and gain as much as I can. I feel that I will be able to walk away with what I have so far, with a lot of gained knowledge and confidence in myself.
D.V.

DANA'S CLASSMATES RESPOND:

Dana is an example of how our love of history affects even our everyday lives. Her interest in the history of Frye Boots and her research being implemented in the corporate model shows that her passion for history is sought out in the most unique ways. Dana is all that is right with a history teacher; her passion for her subject can only translate into a successful teaching profession where students will be engaged and not turned off.

First of all, I have never noticed a scar on Dana's face or head. All I ever noticed was pure, unadulterated beauty. The only thing I would suggest is to be aware of the post-concussive effects, such as headaches and depression. And, you could get a lawyer and sue the parties involved.

I understand your struggles with school growing up. What's amazing is I am still struggling to finish my education, and I'm many years older than you. It is admirable that you say, "I want to help kids who struggle in school and give students the extra push and motivation that they need. I want to make sure I would never make a student feel the way I did growing up and struggle in school." Your parents deserve a big thank you for assisting you with tutors, and encouraging you to pursue your college education.

You also don't just work after school, but you have gotten involved in the company's institutional structure by studying their history and creating a company handbook. Your entrepreneurial skills are readily brought to the forefront of your developing life. Lest we forget, you have developed a positive motivational outlook on life: "I remember one day, thinking to myself in life you go through struggles and hit bumps but you just need to move forward not stop and this will all pass and one day it will just be a memory and something that made you stronger."

I wasn't always the sharpest tool in the shed as they say but I wasn't ever really babied either. I hate to say it but I disagree with your quote that Fred also has in his reply of "I want to help kids who struggle in school..." because it is a dog eat dog world after all. The more people raise their kids to always be protected everywhere they go the more I feel the kids will struggle socially, mentally and even physically. Although it's a part of the growing pains of child, I believe it benefits kids to learn from an early age that there is not always going to be someone assisting you throughout life. There comes a time when you just have to grind it out in any situation whether it be school, work etc.

It is great that you found your initial interest in History through listening to your grandparents' stories about your roots. Although you did not choose to delve into the History major early in your college career, so goes the phrase "better late than never!" It is great that you are even applying the research means you have learned in college to your daily life (for example, the history of the Frye Company)!

I have great respect for Dana's feelings towards children. "I want to help kids who struggle in school and give students the extra push and motivation that they need. I want to make sure I would never make a student feel the way I did growing up and struggle in school." For myself, teaching is a career possibility and this is always something that I wanted to accomplish; not only keeping students interested in the subject, but helping them and making sure they don't fall behind.

Dana is passionate about history. In her early childhood she remembers a song about Christopher Columbus. Dana loved history but in high school the teachers made it boring. This is true. History is such a serious, important and fun subject but some teachers do not have the passion or drive. Dana has the passion and drive to be a different kind of history teacher. She will definitely not be a boring one. Her observations of other teachers in the past will move her away from the boring approach.

(ONCE AGAIN)

UPON A MUSTARD SEED

I was a seed never watered,
Never given intellectual nourishment,
Trying to grow in an environment not meant for me.
Born into a world that's confused
Twitching and turning in a seat, this means I have a learning disability?
Confused world, I am amused world. You have no clue world what to do with a child like me.
Your answer was to give me a disability called ADD, an enemy that I had to defeat.
ADD based off of subjective criteria,
Psychiatrists, teachers, who are you to spread such a disease.
Thanks to you I became the experiment that I never wanted to be.
The environment haunts, leaving scars such as grade marks
The ghost of education's past came to warn

That some teachers and the complete educational system have done children wrong.
It devastates total masses taking away their strength
Weakening, creeping into the spirit ripping the heart from where it belongs
Children learn early whether they are a failure or not due to labels.
From elementary to college the grades don't stop, grades are lies they're not stable
Since I was young I knew I was able.

My age continues to rise I hear the clock, tick tock tick tock
Finally I have arrived at CUNY and ask myself what do I think? Do you really want to know?
I gave it a shot
Everything I thought it would be it was not.
Like elementary and secondary education it leaves you in the same spot
Crippled, fearing the world with no clear vision,
It manipulates your own intuition
Listen
You should be seeking yourself
Your strength, abilities this is the true mission
Find self-definition.
CUNY continues to put you in a spirit ripped, mentally confused, heartless condition.
After CUNY is done it spits you out, abandoned, jobless with no position.
Do not be surprised this is tradition.
Those who accomplished completely, doing what they loved to do, dropped out of school, no college.

They found peace and accomplishment in their own
self –knowledge.

Thomas Edison produced over one thousand
inventions
Kicked out of school because he could not pay
attention
Not to mention
Abraham Lincoln was president of the United States
no degree
He signed the emancipation proclamation setting the
slaves free
He sits in the national mall in Washington D.C
Forever remembered throughout history.
Walt Disney created a land of joy, imagination, movies
with creativity
For all ages no discrimination
Leaving behind his own legacy for generations
No college education.
Albert Einstein genius physicists through hard work
and dedication
He said "The only thing that interferes with my learning is my education."
He failed tests, no stress. He overcame the system
teaching himself in many different ways.
No shame
He saw his purpose his own vision
Looked upon as a failure, Einstein brought out the self-knowledge inside that was hidden.
Bill Gates went to Harvard but had a change of heart.
A prestigious college he could have graduated from but
he did not

The question everyone should ponder is whether a
degree makes you smart?
For Bill he showed the world that labels do not make
you who you are
Getting a piece of paper did not make him or break
him
Cause in the end he found his abilities believing he
would make it.
College can take you but only so far.
It's as if you're a hitchhiker and when you graduate it's
time to get out of the car.
The time you spent inside confined left you blind with
no direction
Finally you start to have some self-reflection.
Seeking your talents, what you love, how to make the
impossible come true.
College teaches you from a very narrow point of view.

So what happened to the seed, did it ever grow?
What gave the seed water, intellectual nourishment?
I really want to know.
It was removing the negative labels that manifested
itself in my life
Learning how to teach myself, putting CUNY aside
Why did I have to pull myself out of the CUNY insti-
tution to actually learn?
I took off a year, time to share what I discerned
Professors with no compassion
Molding the brain by a standard
That for some creates a negative reaction
Grades, GPAs make students unequal
If you have a 2.0 you're banned from entering honor
society clubs

Now this is truly evil.
Who believed that grades and marks make you smart?
Who implemented such a rotten system from the start?
The 2.0 student could be intellectual in so many ways
Instead they're looked at as slow, incapable just because
they don't have the highest grades?
I'm not done
What happens to the 4.0 student who masters every
CUNY class?
Where is he now? I think it's time we asked?
Well he applied for every job he could think of, he
started not to care
He would take anything even if it was a hard job he
had to bear
He busted his hump, day and night studying, getting
the highest grades.
You start to see the 2.0 and 4.0 CUNY student both
deal with inequality in different ways.
It does not fade
The social class structure remains the same
The system is made so you compromise your life for
any job that will pay
Thomas Edison said "Every man makes his own salary"
Could we say this is true today?

CUNY is stamped majority poor and middle class
that's why it's not respected
Those students whether 2.0 or 4.0 most get rejected,
Neglected
The marks, grades labels it is not what you need.
The ultimate knowledge is your-self, your worth, your
purpose.
The faith the size of a mustard seed

So as for Thomas he is right, the salary is yours
As for me getting a degree is just a societal chore
Without it most of your opinions are ignored
So in order to change education, heal it
You have to become the cure
Take out all of the problems all the way to its core
I have just shared my own knowledge to the world of a
system
That should be completely reformed
From the bottom up stop creating inequality for the
American student
If you see they have problems in science, math, English
don't stand there give them an F
Take time out to improve them
Professors, teachers you have to understand, your job is
noble like a nurse in a hospital unit.
Every child counts they all have different ways of
learning,
Sit down master your students
No excuses
Though every professor, teacher is not like this but one
is too many
Infecting a student's life with discouragement is very
deadly
There is no room for error
You're dealing with a human being, spirit, his soul
The infection is some professors, some teachers, the
exams, grades,
The system as a whole
Jesus is god who came down as a man long ago
He gave so many passages of encouragement, telling
man he can achieve the impossible
Faith is important it is a gift

It's hard to fulfill your own purpose without it
So stand up tall declare you believe in yourself
By doing just this you have all the riches and wealth
The wealth that does not exist in school or money just
to look in the mirror and not have to ask
Who are you? You've figured it out, education is life
experience, your dreams, everything you want
pursue
Those who have made it completely, fulfilled a degree
or not are very few
Think about that thought and look inside of you
My mustard seed has grown, it's developed the sky's the
limit
Finally college is over, school is finished
Life continues I'm out of prison
Hopefully, I'll help other students or individuals whose
dreams have been diminished

I'm not bitter nor angry I'm just breaking, exposing
cracking the CUNY shell it's been long overdue
Whether you agree or disagree I'm sharing my personal
view
Allowing the reader to walk in my shoes.

Olivia Porch

28220588R00128

Made in the USA
Lexington, KY
09 December 2013